Missing is a thoughtful and intimate look at life i
ed by borderline personality disorder. Througho
writes with clarity, honesty, and self-awareness--
pity or histrionics.

—Scott Edelstein, *Sex and the Spiritual Teacher*

A candid, riveting account of the author's journey to make sense of a bewildering childhood. With curiosity and compassion, and without blame or bitterness, Ewing shares poignant recollections of being raised by a parent with
borderline personality disorder in a way that feels as though we're walking
beside her. We are right there as she revisits perplexing experiences, honestly
looks at her relationships with her own children and, ultimately, arrives at a
new and lighter place, one of deeper understanding, acceptance and peace.

—Kimberlee Roth, co-author, *Surviving a Borderline Parent*

This is a vivid, stirring, deeply informative book about coming to terms with
a mother with a devastating mental illness. Kathy Ewing writes with grace,
generosity and—always—heartstopping candor.

—Marian Sandmaier, *Original Kin: The Search for Connection Among Adult
Sisters and Brothers; The Invisible Alcoholics: Women and Alcohol*

Compelling and beautifully written.

—Barbara Finn, PhD, Clinical Psychologist, Menlo Park, California

Kathy Ewing unconfuses the science regarding borderline personality disorder, which can be murky and confounding, even for therapists. Most stories
about BPD focus on the drama, but the brilliance of Ewing's narrative is stepping around the quick and easy to show emptiness, hunger, and hopelessness
as the driving forces in her mother's psyche, as well as their powerful impact
on her baffled, resourceful kid. At the same time, she evokes a small-town
'50s childhood pitch perfectly. This book will help a lot of people who grew
up in similar circumstances make sense of their experience and move past it.
Kathy Ewing is a hero.

—Belleruth Naparstek, *Invisible Heroes: Survivors of Trauma and How They
Heal;* creator of the Health Journeys guided imagery audio series

Missing:

Coming to Terms with a Borderline Mother

By Kathy Ewing

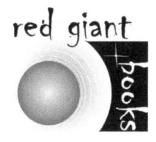

Someone I loved once gave me
A box full of darkness.
It took me years to understand
That this, too, was a gift.

-- Mary Oliver

Introduction: About Borderline Personality Disorder

Books about depression and schizophrenia fill the shelves of bookstores and libraries. Autism and bipolar disorder have inspired hundreds of volumes. We've been inundated with self-help manuals, medical advice books, and memoirs by patients and loved ones affected by these diseases. A shelf devoted to borderline personality disorder (BPD), in contrast, would contain a small number of mostly jargon-laden tomes targeted at professionals. Few are geared toward a popular audience, and even fewer are memoirs. Only two concern borderline parents.

It's surprising, then, to learn how prevalent BPD is. Until recently, experts estimated that 2 to 3 percent of Americans and 20 percent of psychiatric outpatients suffer from BPD—over seven million people. A recent study has upped the estimate to an astounding 6 percent. That would total around eighteen million Americans, more than three times the number of Alzheimer's patients. (Schizophrenia and bipolar disorder each occur in about 1 percent of the population.) Reporting on this study in 2009, *Time* called BPD our age's "signature crack-up illness." In 2005, *O Magazine* featured BPD—a sure sign of the disorder's coming out of the shadows. When you factor in family members affected by the disease, the numbers are as high as thirty million people or more.

When I began to connect my mother's enigmatic, frustrating behavior with BPD, I read everything I could find hoping to understand her. Most of the books contained wise and compassionate descriptions of this very complex disease, but very little about borderline parents. The word "mother" in the indexes nearly always referred to the patient's mother, and the author often blamed her for causing the patient's problems.

Then I ran across Christine Ann Lawson's *Understanding the Borderline Mother: Helping Her Children Transcend the Intense, Unpredictable, and Volatile Relationship*. Lawson uses fairy-tale characters as archetypes for the mother with BPD: the waif, the hermit, the queen, and the witch. Lawson's vivid descriptions and tremendous empathy for family members helped me, but my mother didn't fit into Lawson's neat categories. As I struggled toward forgiving my mother, Lawson's condemnations of the borderline mother, though sometimes gratifying, came to seem too harsh.

Eventually, I found *Surviving a Borderline Parent: How to Heal Your Childhood Wounds and Build Trust, Boundaries, and Self-Esteem* by Kimberlee Roth and Freda B. Friedman, with a foreword by Randi Kreger. I devoured this book in one sitting. The first chapter, "I Never Knew It Had a Name," expressed my feelings exactly; I'd finally found a name for my mother's anger, unhappiness, and seeming irrationality.

BPD is a frustratingly variable, hard-to-pin-down phenomenon. "These patients . . . are a heterogeneous group . . . Even the same patient will present with a wide variety of problems at different times," says Arthur Freeman, editor of *Comparative Treatments for Borderline Personality Disorder*. Another specialist, Robert G. Harper, describes patients as sometimes relatively pleasant, engaging, and responsive, while at other times depressed, sullen, confused, disorganized, angry, demanding, drug-seeking, or manipulative. These various manifestations represent different aspects, or different combinations, of the borderline personality.

Certain symptoms, though, are hallmarks of the disorder. A person with BPD forms intense relationships and tries frantically to prevent the other person from abandoning her. (Traditionally, three times as many women have been diagnosed with BPD as men, but the recent "6-percent study" suggests a roughly even ratio between the genders.) This neediness, in a terrible irony, often drives the other person away. When that idealized person inevitably falls short, the BPD sufferer suddenly reverses her high opinion, and the other person is no longer loved, but despised. The professionals call this process "idealization versus devaluation," or "splitting." The person on whom they're focusing all of their energies becomes either a devil or an angel.

These extreme shifts show up in other aspects of borderline thinking. People with BPD often are unable to see shades of gray. Black-and-white thinking causes them to feel that they're in the worst possible situation, that they're in more pain than anyone else in the world, and that they'll trust therapy only if it cures them completely—at which time they'll be completely happy, like the people they imagine surround them. The emotions of people with BPD are erratic, although, as one writer puts it, the moods tend to veer wildly from bad to very bad. Rage is one salient symptom, and studies show that a high percentage of men incarcerated for violent crimes have borderline personality disorder.

The term "borderline," coined in 1938 by psychoanalyst Adolph Stern, describes a middle ground between neurosis and psychosis. These Freudian categories are nearly obsolete now, but the borderline between the two suggests that BPD is more challenging than a neurosis such as a phobia, but less debilitating than a psychotic illness like schizophrenia, in which a patient suffers hallucinations and loses touch with reality. Controversy surrounds the term, which has accumulated negative connotations due to the difficulty in treating the disorder. Some researchers have found strong neurobiological evidence for BPD. Some trace borderline symptoms to a childhood trauma, such as abuse, resulting in a sense of emptiness and a lack of a strong sense of self. BPD might then be a manifestation of post-traumatic stress disorder. Others make connections with attachment disorders. Lacking a sense of self, the patient may resort to impulsive activities, like excessive spending or sexual acting out, to fill the void. She has difficulty feeling empathy. It's very hard for her to imagine what it's like to be someone else. Some sources suggest that Marilyn Monroe, Princess Diana, Joan Crawford, and Mary Todd

Lincoln may have suffered from BPD.

The jargon used to describe these symptoms is sometimes daunting, but it's not just the language that makes them hard to understand. It's also the chaotic and inconsistent nature of BPD itself. At first glance, the symptoms don't seem to mesh; they have no apparent logic. When you get to know a person with the disorder, however, the symptoms make a crazy sense. "When explored in depth," says Jerold J. Kreisman in *I Hate You—Don't Leave Me: Understanding the Borderline Personality*, ". . . symptoms are seen to be intricately connected, interacting with each other so that one symptom sparks the rise of another like the pistons of a combustion engine."

A pervasive feeling of emptiness makes the person with BPD want to fill the emptiness with anything—say, an extravagant shopping spree or a one-night stand. That empty feeling also makes her latch onto relationships and then cling desperately to them, terrified that she will be abandoned. To fill the emptiness, she invents identities for herself, but because she doesn't really know who she is, the emotions are chaotic and generally angry. Because she has trouble empathizing with others, she resents them for not meeting her needs. Other times she merely feels empty.

Much of the literature presents BPD's prognosis as dire. Dr. Richard Moskovitz, in *Lost in the Mirror: An Inside Look at Borderline Personality Disorder*, suggests that one in ten adult women suffer from BPD, most of them undiagnosed. Even when diagnosed, many patients quit therapy because the therapist, like everyone else, disappoints them. In some cases, the therapist blames the patient and takes the patient's lack of progress personally. Unlike depression or schizophrenia, BPD seems resistant to medication, though some medications ameliorate certain symptoms. The disorder's causes are not clear, but most therapists assume that there is some genetic or biological predisposition working alongside environmental triggers.

New therapies are offering hope, however. Dr. Marsha Linehan, director of the Behavioral Research and Therapy Clinics at the University of Washington, has developed a promising treatment for BPD called dialectical behavior therapy. Linehan focus-

4

es on the inability to regulate emotion properly. Sometimes, she writes, people with BPD habitually suppress painful emotions ("inhibited grieving") because they don't have the tools to handle them. The therapist must directly confront, in a caring and accepting manner, the patients' emotions and dysfunctional behavior. Linehan's compassionate approach involves reassuring patients that the therapist won't abandon them and trying whenever possible to validate their feelings instead of contradicting them. Her approach also requires therapists to work together to share the stresses of their work and honestly to face their own frustrations and emotions. I explore Linehan's theories in greater detail at the end of this book.

"Consider what it must be like to be raised by a borderline parent," muses Dr. John G. Gunderson in *Imbroglio: Rising to the Challenges of Borderline Personality Disorder,* Janice M. Cauwels's 1992 study of BPD. People with borderline personality disorder are unhappy. They experience "a pervasive pattern of instability in interpersonal relationships, self-image and emotions." Dr. Rex W. Cowdry describes their characteristic unhappiness as a mix of "depression, emptiness, anxiety, varying degrees of rage . . . sort of a tumultuous inner state"

I know what it's like to be raised by someone variously sullen, pleasant, angry, demanding, manipulative, engaging, and all the rest—sometimes changing from one mood to the next in a single conversation. I have begun my story by setting down memories from my childhood, in rough chronology, showing my mother's troubling behavior—the behavior that mystified me until I found a name for it, until I could put it in the context of BPD. As the story continues into my adulthood, the chronology pretty much disappears. In the second part of the book, I move back and forth in time, trying to connect the borderline dots, relating my aging mother's behavior to the symptoms that I now am trying to understand. At last, I try to show how the diagnosis, the wrestling with our history, and the writing have provided some comfort, if not healing.

Helping me along the way is a friend whom I call Nancy. Her

struggles with BPD set me on the path to learning about the illness and helped explain the disorder and my mother to me. The details of her life have been changed to protect her privacy. In adding this book to the short BPD shelf, I hope other adult children will find a name for the confusion in which they grew up, gain some understanding of this perplexing disease, and find a source of reflection for their own experience with a borderline parent.

Part I: Scenes from Childhood

Liz attempted her first sketch of her mother, her first outline for the outside world of the domestic ghost with which she had lived so long.

Margaret Drabble, *The Radiant Way*

Prologue

When the dog died, my mom showed no reaction that I can remember. I don't remember her speaking of it at all until days later. My sister and I commiserated with each other; I know Marge felt as bad as I did—probably worse, because she was older and it was sort of her dog, and she felt more responsible for having let him run loose. We cried and cried and talked it over in the days that followed.

It happened at night. Snap had gone missing, and Marge was outside calling him, but he didn't come home. She told me later that she thought she actually knew when it happened. She imagined that her calling his name had lured him, running home, into the path of a truck.

Marge must have found him the next morning, lying by the side of the road across from our house. I am ashamed to recall that his body lay there for days. My dad, a paraplegic, couldn't dig a grave from his wheelchair. Marge and I, then only about twelve and eight years old, didn't know what to do. That my mother might take some action never entered our heads. Eventually, our neighbor Mr. Dill dug a hole in his yard and buried our dog. No one—not my father, my sister or me, not my mother—said anything about what needed to be done about our dog lying by the side of the road. We were in the habit of not saying anything about painful subjects.

This loss was a very ordinary tragedy. What child doesn't have to deal with the death of a pet? but why, over forty years later, is it still such a dark and painful memory?

A few days after Snap died, my mother hovered around the dinner table, carrying food and avoiding eye contact with my sister and me. Then, seeming to be continuing some conversation they'd had, she abruptly said this to my father: "It happened because they always let the dog run loose. We told them not to let it run loose."

My father, who rarely showed impatience with my mother, shushed her and said, "I thought we agreed not to say anything like that."

That was the only conversation, the only words spoken by my mother about Snap's dying. As I recall scenes from my childhood, this incident seems typical. My mother was often absent or, at least, emotionally absent. She responded inappropriately, if at all. Although she was physically at home most of the time, she was rarely present.

Thirty years later, I'm standing in my own backyard with my kids on a sunny afternoon. Our goldfish died, and we put him in a box, dug a hole, and prepared a little service. My daughter Margaret, about four years old, clings to my leg sobbing. I stroke her hair and lean down to hug her now and then. She cries and cries. I whisper to her, "I'm sorry you feel so bad. It's okay, Margaret." After our makeshift funeral, she feels much better. I'm amazed how quickly she recovers.

Ah, I think to myself, this might have helped. A hug. A comforting word. This is what was missing.

Beginnings

It seems to me now that I spent my childhood passive and absorbent as a sponge. Like all children, I observed closely; I took things in. I didn't analyze. I didn't compare. People said I was quiet. Most of the time, I didn't know what to say. I soaked up who my family was and carried it around with me, as I still do. I identified with each person I observed, slowly beginning a long history as go-between, negotiator, and interpreter of one person to another person.

I realized one crucial thing: my dad's illness made us different. No one else's dad was in a wheelchair, as far as I knew. Even then, throughout my childhood, I knew that my father's illness was the defining fact of our family life. We circled around it, silently, like the dark closet that formed the center of our house.

So, even though this is mostly a story of me and my mom

and how I have come to understand her, I'm starting somewhere else, with something that happened before I can remember. I'm starting with what happened to my dad.

It began with a backache. Believing he had merely strained his back while painting our house and seeing no need for medical advice, my father bought an electric heating pad to ease his discomfort. I store this pad even now deep in my linen closet under the sheets, as a somber artifact of that time. It was 1953, and I was two years old.

When my dad finally saw the doctor, the diagnosis was polio. My sisters and I were vaccinated, and everyone who visited my dad had to wear a mask and gown. When the treatment for polio had no effect and the symptoms worsened, the doctors realized they had made a mistake.

They discovered an abscess on my dad's spine that had damaged his spinal cord. Surgery relieved the abscess, but further damaged his spinal cord. He came home determined to walk again with the help of crutches. A cumbersome set of parallel bars sat in his room, along with a pair of braces with which to train. After several years of struggle, he was forced into a dreadful decision. Because he suffered pain and muscle spasms, the doctors recommended further surgery in which the nerves of his spinal cord above the waist would be severed, leaving him with no feeling or movement in his legs.

Spinal cord. Abscess. Paraplegic. These words were passed on to me; I accepted this story on faith, but always wondered how accurate the medical details were. One evening several years ago, sitting next to a friendly neurologist at a dinner party, I felt comfortable questioning him. I tried the words, one after another. Abscess. Paralysis. Did we have the story right? Was it plausible? It was, he told me kindly. In the early 1950s, he said, the misdiagnosis, the abscess, the drastic surgery all would have made sense.

After the second, decisive surgery, which removed any hope of walking again, my father underwent two solid years of rehabilitation and training at New York's renowned Institute of Physical Medicine and Rehabilitation (now called the Rusk Institute of Rehabilitation Medicine). When he returned home, he was in a wheelchair for good. I was six years old.

All this time, my mother remained back home in Canton, Ohio, alone with three little girls. She received no counseling and no therapy. Friends and family provided some support, and the local newspaper where my dad worked, *The Repository*, continued to pay his salary. Its parent company, Brush-Moore Newspapers, generously took care of his medical expenses, including flying him to New York on their private plane. But my mother's husband had disappeared, and when he returned, he wasn't the man he had been. He was, as we used to say, handicapped.

In the way of that time, he stayed home. Because he was unable to go to work, the paper allowed him to do some writing from home. For about a decade he wrote a weekly column called "Letters from Max" and culled old stories of interest from *Repository* microfilm files for a column called "Up Through a Century." For the rest of his life, our income remained at his 1953 level, about $5,000 a year. Each night at bedtime, he shifted from his wheelchair to the stairs and painstakingly pulled himself up backwards, using his arms and shoulders, step by step, and carefully eased his way down the stairs every morning. Later my parents added a first-floor bedroom and bath for my dad, but my mom continued to sleep upstairs. My parents' sexual relationship, as far as I know, ended.

Hard changes. Thinking about my mother, I try to keep her travails in perspective. My sisters and I repeat these mantras: He had counseling, she had none. She lost a strong, active husband. They had considered having another baby, which was now out of the question. And so on.

I also try to be fair by remembering what my mother did right. Despite everything, she could laugh sometimes, and she made our meals and got us to school and did many of the things mothers do. Even so, her unhappiness is what all of us remember best. My sisters and I wonder if her mental illness, if that's what it was, was precipitated by my dad's "abandonment" in 1953.

Many times, in my father's presence, my mother pointedly

referred to herself as a widow.

My father's wheelchair was a presence in our house—an object to squeeze past at the kitchen table, heave into the back of the station wagon, and wheel around in at a breakneck pace when Dad was in bed. It was big and heavy, like a 1950s car, and had a red leather seat and back. To me, the chair was a part of my father. He set his beer down in the corner of the seat next to his right hip and draped his leg over the armrest while he watched TV, sometimes with me on his lap.

My father was a paraplegic for the last twenty years of his life and about the first twenty years of mine, from the early 1950s to his death from cancer in 1971. Paralyzed from just above the waist down, he had the use only of his chest and arm muscles. Although he could maneuver the wheelchair around the house and get in and out of bed by himself, he had to ask my sisters or me for help whenever he wanted to go outdoors.

Sometimes, when he asked, we would sigh. Then we would back him up to the side door and roll him down the ramp a neighbor had built for him onto the side porch. After a sharp right pivot, we rolled him backwards off the porch and onto the rough grass of the backyard.

He wasn't a small man. The chair rocked heavily from side to side, bumping off the porch and over the grass. Sometimes it was easier to tilt it way back and let the large rear wheels take all the weight. Once, moving from the porch to the backyard, I somehow tipped over the chair, with my father in it. I panicked, while my dad, lying on the grass, was a little grumpy but calm. I ran to get a neighbor, who came to help. My mother remained somewhere in the house, ostensibly unaware and studiously uninvolved.

In the winter, the wheelchair dug into the snow and slush and skidded a little. Getting out to the driveway took extra finesse, requiring the pressure of my foot on the rear of the chair for traction. No wonder that back then, as my father often pointed out, many disabled people mostly stayed indoors during the winter. My dad, resolutely independent, had hand controls installed in the car so that he could drive.

Determined to get out of the house, he took us on a couple

of driving vacations. We went from Canton to Niagara Falls in 1960. Finding a motel that could accommodate a wheelchair was a major struggle. My dad would pull into a likely place. Betsey, my oldest sister, would run inside and ask the manager, and she'd run back out to say, no, their doorways weren't wide enough. At one place, the manager assured us that his place was accessible. We unloaded my dad and the luggage and went inside, only to find that my dad's chair couldn't fit through the bathroom door. We had to load everything back into the car to search for another motel.

Betsey was eight years older than I, and about sixteen at the time. She always bore most of the responsibility for moving my dad around, with the help of Marge, who is four years younger than Betsey. I didn't take over until much later. For several years, Betsey helped Dad go to a chess club in the city, and sometimes she played with him and the other members. I don't remember my mom ever pushing the wheelchair or trying to load it into the car. My dad said that she had enough to bear, and so, any task that we kids could do, we had to do. At home it was always one of us who helped him in and out of the house.

In nice weather, going outside often meant playing catch. Thus, my father saved us three girls from lifelong embarrassment in neighborhood softball games. Playing catch was a kind of drill, my dad alternating pop-ups, grounders, and line drives. I can still picture his throw—all arm, overhand, rocking his powerless legs and hips. We girls learned to catch and throw, and you have to throw accurately to a guy in a wheelchair. If you missed by only a little and the ball landed right next to the chair, my father could reach down and get it, but if it landed a few feet away, we'd have to retrieve it ourselves. With a really wild throw, into the shrubs or trees, my father would look bewildered and joke, "Who was that to?"

I don't remember my mom ever coming outside with us. I don't ever remember her pulling up a chair to watch us play, or walking around the yard, or looking at the garden, or pulling weeds. All I remember is her absence.

When the sun set and the air grew colder, it was time to go

back inside. I'd grab the white plastic handles on the back of the chair and push hard up the slope to the porch. I'd tilt the chair back a little to lift the front wheels onto the concrete porch and then raise the heavy back wheels. Then we'd turn sharp to the left and align the wheels with the ramp. Pushing the chair up the ramp took strength, but my dad could stop the wheels with his hands to keep from rolling backwards if I had to pause for breath on the way. With the final push into the dining room he'd take over himself. And always, he'd say thank you.

The wheelchair is merely the most visible encumbrance of paraplegics, not necessarily the biggest burden or hardship. To able-bodied people, not walking seems the worst thing, because they don't suspect paraplegia's other complications. Like many other paraplegics, my dad had to wear a urinary catheter at all times. All day, his urine drained into a bag that hung down his leg inside his trousers. At night, or when he was ill, the catheter drained into an old glass milk bottle that sat beside his bed. He emptied it regularly, or, when he was sick, my mom did. As a child, I didn't understand all the mysterious medical paraphernalia in my dad's bathroom. Though my parents protected us from these medical details, I emptied that urine bottle occasionally. The pungent odor in my dad's bedroom didn't repel me: it was connected to my dad, familiar and part of our household.

Because of the catheter, my dad was prone to urinary infections and was careful to drink lots of liquids to prevent them. He was also vulnerable to other fleeting infections that would make his temperature spike. He was often stuck in bed, drinking fluids, trying to bring his temperature down.

None of these concerns embarrassed me. He was my dad, and this was the way things were. I took a certain pride in his different-ness, aware, even as a young kid, that friends and neighbors admired his mettle. At the same time, I felt deeply for him, knew that my mom was bitter and troubled, and recognized that I was missing out on an able-bodied, active father. Every birthday, before I blew out the candles on my cake, I wished that my dad would be able to walk again. Every night I prayed that he would get well.

Like the wheelchair, my dad's parallel bars occasionally became a plaything. Huge, heavy iron bars attached to a rough wooden floor remained in his bedroom along with the torturous, heavy leg braces, even several years after his death. When I was little, I read a book about Native Americans that described the Navajo dwellings called hogans. I created my own hogan by draping blankets over the parallel bars. I could crawl into my shelter and then arrange my dolls in makeshift beds along one side. I set up play dishes and furniture. In half-light, I enacted family dramas with my dolls, all alone. Sometimes my dad lay in bed nearby where he could hear me whispering to my dolls. Most times he was up and about, while I played alone in his room. He always spoke fondly of the "hoe-gan," stressing the last syllable for comedic effect.

Bedsores, or decubitus ulcers, also plague those with paraplegia. Pressure sores. My dad often worried about a red spot here or there on his body that he would have to watch to make sure it didn't turn into a real wound. In bed, he had to change position frequently, and in his chair, he sat on various pillows to change the pressure on his skin. Because he had no feeling in his lower extremities, he had to use a mirror to check his back and backside for spots, or ask my mother to do it.

In 1967, some of these inflammations gradually developed into serious ulcers. My dad had to return to New York for skin grafts and long rehabilitation to repair ugly bedsores. He was gone for my sophomore year in high school, and he missed my sister Betsey's wedding. He underwent several surgeries.

My father dealt with all his difficulties and indignities stalwartly, but he never pretended not to be bothered. Once I naively asked if his upper body was stronger than it had been before his illness. He snapped, "Of course not." Stung, I explained that all that hauling himself in and out of the car and bed might have just strengthened his arms and shoulders. He softened, acknowledged the possibility, but repeated, "No. In no way am I as strong as I was." In fact, he felt more susceptible in every way to illness. His resistance to all diseases had been compromised.

He also lacked physical balance. He told a story about some aides at the New York hospital who dropped him on the floor, not believing that he couldn't hold himself up. He had to be vigilant about his legs and feet, checking for wounds. I was impressed by his admonitions to us that pain is actually good—a difficult concept for a child to comprehend. He told me once about a patient in New York who had placed a boiling pot of water on his lap and never realized how terribly burned he was until he undressed that night. That thought horrified me for years.

He told many stories of New York. Some concerned Fred Hawkins, a practical nurse who had become his friend. Fred was black, which fascinated me, since I knew no black people. They corresponded after Dad came home, and he described Fred as the most capable and compassionate nurse he had met. I remember his stunned and sad expression when he learned that Fred had died of a heart attack. He also got to know Drs. Donald A. Covalt and Howard A. Rusk, founders of the Institute and innovators in the care of people with disabilities. He saw Roy Campanella in the Institute halls, the Brooklyn Dodgers catcher whose career was cut short by the 1958 car accident that left him paralyzed. He became friends with Mark Di Suvero, the noted sculptor, whom my dad called a "beatnik," because of his beard and ratty turtleneck. I still have a quick, rough, abstract painting on newsprint that Di Suvero did for my dad. I've looked for the letters from Di Suvero, but suspect my mother heedlessly threw them away after my dad's death.

She also seems to have discarded letters from Alger Hiss, the Roosevelt State Department official accused of spying, whose case ushered in the Red Scare of the 1950s. Through a mutual friend, Hiss arranged to visit my dad regularly in the hospital in 1967, and they remained in touch when he came home. In reading about Hiss in the intervening years, I've learned that he made a habit of visiting people who were alone in the city. He must have discerned the importance of visitors from his incarceration in the federal penitentiary in Lewisburg, Pennsylvania, from 1951 to 1954. In *Laughing Last*, a biography by his son Tony, he is quoted as saying, "I love to visit people in the hospital," and I felt he was speaking directly to me about visiting my dad.

These exotic contacts interested me. My dad never name-dropped, but he enjoyed getting to know people and learned from their experience and suffering. He took care to maintain his relationships via letters and phone calls.

In contrast, my mother had no friends. She rarely wrote letters. She never went out to lunch or a movie. She never chatted on the phone. She didn't get her hair done or go shopping for fun. When my sisters and I began driving, my mother gradually stopped. She spent more and more time sitting in front of the TV.

In 1964, my dad began trying to form a club for handicapped people. At that time, accessibility was nonexistent, and disabled people were pretty much stuck at home. He wrote letters to the editors of newspapers in several nearby towns proposing a social organization. One such letter began, "In Stark County, there must be scores of severely handicapped persons who do not get much recreation and who would enjoy belonging to a group formed for this purpose--if only there were such an organization." The Handicapped Club (later more elegantly called the Handicapped Association) began meeting several months later and continued for years. Often, we picked people up at their homes and brought them to meetings when they had no family members to help them. The group would play cards, socialize, have a meal, and sometimes visit a park together. Two members, Nancy and Leroy, both in wheelchairs, met at a meeting and eventually married.

Around that time, State Representative Bernice McKenzie appointed my dad to a commission to study disability issues, including accessibility. He wrote letters and talked with her on the phone. I think he played some small part in the movement toward the Americans with Disabilities Act, enacted in 1990, which guaranteed, among other things, the removal of physical barriers to people with disabilities.

Although my father's paraplegia caused immeasurable grief in our family, it made my sisters and me stronger and more competent. We learned to fix, carry, and move things that my dad couldn't fix, carry, or move. We learned to throw and catch. My father drove us on long trips, continued to work for the newspaper, helped my mother around the house and us with our homework, wrote frequent letters to friends, helped other disabled people, and taught us how valiantly a person could deal with adversity. At his funeral, I remember some old friends saying, as people will at funerals, that his death was "for the best." If they meant that it was just as well that his final illness had ended, I suppose they were right. But I was pretty sure they meant it was good thing his long suffering in a wheelchair was over, and I couldn't help thinking they were also wishing away the only father I ever knew.

The Neighborhood

One day, when I was little, my mother and I walked to the Rices' house, which sat behind ours at the end of a long lane that served as their driveway. My mother carried a casserole dish.

Mrs. Rice was sitting up in her bed, smiling and friendly. I hardly knew her, seeing her only when she drove by our house, or when we visited on Halloween. In her bed, she looked pale and thin. She wore a loose sleeveless nightgown that revealed a huge jagged scar on her right arm, snaking under her nightgown toward her chest. We stayed a little while, chatting. A few months later, Mrs. Rice died of breast cancer.

That's the only time I remember my mother calling on a neighbor and the only time I know of that she reached out in kindness to any of them.

We lived in a white frame house just outside of Canton in a rural area gradually transforming into suburbia. It sat on a half-acre, a yard that, looking back, now seems like Tara to me, a city dweller with a small lot. Our entire backyard served as my dad's garden before he got sick—"sick" being our family locution for what had happened to him. He had grown cabbages and corn, tomatoes, squash, and pumpkins, in harvests so great that my mother would can and freeze much of the bounty. Large earthenware crocks sat in our basement, where my parents had made sauerkraut from cabbage. This fruitful garden, along with my mother's standing over boiling pots of vegetables, became mythic in my mind. Like our old dog Chipper (before Snap), like my dad walking, the garden was something I believed in rather than remembered.

To me, even some of our current neighbors seemed part of a mythic past. I knew my sisters played with the Schells down the street, but I had barely ever seen them. The Rice kids behind us were older and sophisticated, like my sister Betsey, glamorous and mysterious to me. I knew the Walkers, the gentle elderly couple right next door. Mr. Walker grew spectacular rows of tulips and lilies, and when my dad was outside, Mr. Walker would come over, and they'd chat about growing things. The Walkers had lost their son, their only child, in a car accident years before, and I understood that Mrs. Walker's grief had made her forgetful and confused.

We were closest to the Dills, who lived on the other side of us and owned a couple of acres that included a pond, a place for skating in winter and swimming in the summer, though we avoided the end of the pond where snapping turtles resided. Joe Dill acted as a courier for my dad—delivering his finished columns to the *Repository,* and bringing back the microfilms of old papers that my dad scoured for his "Up Through a Century" column. Mr. Dill worked at the paper as a printer. His wife Nancy didn't have a job, except for the short time she ran a cozy, inviting yarn shop in their basement. She tried to make some extra money by teaching knitting and selling yarn and other supplies. She taught my sister Marge and me how to knit. The Dills' son Chuck, around Marge's age, was mentally retarded, the term used at the time for his condition. Our neighborhood playmate, he spent lots of time in our yard with Marge and me and our pack of neighborhood dogs. As an adult, Marge continued to see Chuck for many years, treating him to dinner once a month.

Mr. Dill—a jovial, grey-haired, good-hearted man, a little older than my parents—would sometimes take Marge, Chuck, and me out for ice cream or to the bowling alley. I imagine now that he wanted to give us something to do, as well as provide a social life for his son. For some reason, I had the impression that Mr. Dill wasn't very smart and maybe a little naïve and that people might easily take advantage of him.

Mrs. Dill seemed cannier. She had a hearty laugh and a wicked sense of humor, handsome blue eyes and elegant salt-and-pepper hair pulled back in a loose bun. It seemed to me that her husband's innocence sometimes made her a little impatient. Although she was usually genial, there was a bitterness about her—a sense of failure, I think, about their child's disability. Both Dills were welcoming to us, and Mrs. Dill was especially close to Marge. I loved their big rambling house, lived-in but not cluttered like ours, and their dog Laddie and cat Cleo as though they were my own. I loved Mrs. Dill's spicy cinnamon hermit cookies at Christmas time. Though I wouldn't have touched cookies with nuts and raisins at home, at the Dill house they tasted homey and comforting.

Despite their warmth, I grew up feeling that the Dills were the unluckiest family I knew. Raising Chuck was a challenge. He never learned to read, kids made fun of him, and he suffered lots of health problems.

Their money-making schemes never worked out. They built a solid brick building on the wooded corner of their property we called the pine grove. It housed the knitting shop for awhile and then was intended to become what Mr. Dill called a Fishing Club, and he stocked the pond with trout, which all died before any fishermen showed up. Later in life, Mr. Dill suffered from heart disease, and his leg was amputated. Mrs. Dill had a mental break-down, requiring several hospitalizations.

At least one of their efforts to make extra income panned out, however. They split their big house into apartments. The upstairs could accommodate a family, and a little efficiency apartment off to the side worked well for a single person.

For a while an Englishwoman named Kathleen rented this space. Mrs. Dill and Kathleen used to come over to our house on an occasional Friday evening to play bridge. Kathleen was a trim, sedate young woman, in her thirties, who taught at an exclusive private school in town. Cordial but reserved, she could relax enough to laugh at my dad's jokes, which endeared her to me. When the Beatles first appeared on Ed Sullivan in 1964, my dad asked her what she thought of them. She shuddered, visibly disgusted, and muttered, "Those accents!"

I was relieved when both Mrs. Dill and Kathleen came for bridge, because then I didn't have to play. My only duty was to make coffee for the four adults, which I enjoyed. We almost never brewed coffee at our house, so my job was to boil water and pour it over instant coffee. We had a brown carafe for the coffee, which I brought into the living room and poured into mugs. It was probably horrible coffee, but they all thanked and complimented me anyway.

But when Kathleen didn't come, our parents drafted one of us girls to fill in as the fourth. Serving as Mrs. Dill's or my dad's bridge partner was not so bad. Through the long, tedious games, I could derive pleasure, sometimes, in learning the game's rudiments and winning the occasional unexpected trick. At nine or ten, I hadn't mastered the intricacies of bidding, and I never did, for lack of interest. I never counted cards as they were played. Hence, I made frequent mistakes. Dad and Mrs. Dill explained strategy to me, complimented me when I did something right, and rarely pointed out my errors. I think they realized I was only a child.

Serving as my mom's bridge partner was another story. She maintained a formal politeness; she never ranted or raved. She also never made eye contact. An experienced bridge player, she would send a clear signal in bidding that would be lost on me. Then she'd look at the other adults and shake her head impatiently, or sigh deeply. Often when I played what I thought was an appropriate card, she would purse her lips and shake her head. When I'd lay my dummy hand down on the table, my mom might exclaim with dismay, "Why didn't you bid hearts?" and I knew I'd blown it. At least as the dummy, I could watch her play the cards instead of making my own risky choices. If we made our bid, I felt relieved that my mother was happy, but mostly I just hoped the game would end soon without my mother expressing too much impatience or disappointment.

Neither my sisters nor I play bridge as adults. My husband has tried for thirty years to get me to play Hearts with him and our children. Hearts, he says, is much simpler than bridge. But I hear the word "trump" and see tricks getting collected, and for thirty years I've told him that I'd rather not.

Seen from a certain angle, my childhood was a series of small-scale horror shows, at least in the pet department. Snap, hit by a car, was preceded by my family's archetypal pet Chipper. There's a photograph of my dad before his illness, standing behind me as a toddler and holding Chipper's collar. In family lore, Chipper ran away. I've always wondered if he escaped while my dad was hospitalized in New York or soon after he returned home. These were times when nobody around our house would have been paying much attention to the dog.

Then, when I was about five, there was the kitten with a hole in its neck. I don't know where the kitten came from. I don't know why it had a hole in its neck—whether it was congenital or from some sort of infection. What I remember best is that a nurse friend of my father's, a woman who had taken care of him and was visiting us, took a look at the kitten. I remember her gentle face and calm voice as she explained that the kitten probably wouldn't survive, and we probably needn't bother taking it to the vet. This bad news was delivered with such kindness that it's a warm memory rather than an awful one.

Another kitten died a violent death in our front yard. My sister's friend Joyce was visiting us with her new dog. The dog regarded our kitten as a plaything, as dogs sometimes do. She picked it up and, like a predator with its prey, shook it to death. I escaped to the basement and hid there in shock. I think Marge came after me and coaxed me out.

In all these stories, my mother was around somewhere, hovering in the wings. She played no actual part in these dramas.

Snap came next, short for Gingersnap, for his warm reddish-brown color. He was a smallish mutt, a beagle mix that Marge received for her birthday. Against my mother's wishes, my dad drove her to the pound to pick out a dog. During that summer, I would lie next to Snap on our side porch, stroking him and singing my favorite song from school, "Where Go the Boats," from this Robert Louis Stevenson poem:

Dark brown is the river.
Golden is the sand.
It flows along for ever,
With trees on either hand.

Green leaves a-floating,
Castles of the foam,
Boats of mine a-boating—
Where will all come home?

On goes the river,
And out past the mill,
Away down the valley,
Away down the hill.

Away down the river,
A hundred miles or more,
Other little children
Shall bring my boats ashore.

When I found these lyrics online, I went to the piano to pick out the melody. The tune evokes all the feelings of loving that dog that summer.

When I was older, we acquired some rabbits. Marge, the animal lover, had sneaked the two of us into a 4-H club against our parents' better judgment. Our first projects were sheep, then a couple of goats (mine), then rabbits. The sheep and goats did fine because we kept them at my grandfather's, about ten minutes away in more rural Louisville. The unfortunate bunnies we housed in makeshift hutches in the backyard. The whole enterprise was pretty much a disaster. Occasionally the rabbits would escape into our big yard, where our latest dog, Abbie, and the neighbor dogs Laddie and Sarge, hung out. They chased Sam, a New Zealand White, around the yard one day, and Marge and I ran after them, screaming for them to stop. We finally caught the dogs, but Sam lay panting under one of our evergreens and died there, apparently of exhaustion. A favorite, adorable, lop-eared rabbit named Thumper escaped from his cage and was hit by a car. To make matters worse, after we buried the rabbits, one dog or another would dig them up and leave the carnage strewn around the yard.

Another bunny named Lucy gave birth to about ten little pink hairless babies scattered around her cage. Some of them fell through the spaces in the wire floor to the grass below. We got my dad outside to help put the litter to rights, but while Marge had run inside to get a box for them and I was collecting them, I accidentally stepped on one and killed it. Dad shouted at me to look out, but it was too late. A terrible thing to happen to a guilt-prone little girl. That night, crying, I told Marge what I had done, and she comforted me.

It never occurred to me to seek out my mother for comfort, or to tell her what had happened, or to ask her for help. During all the mayhem, she was probably puttering in the kitchen, doing laundry in the basement, or reading magazines. She was somewhere around, but AWOL, ghostlike, and disengaged.

Home

Even now, when I'm falling asleep and when I'm waking, the household in my mind—the arrangement of rooms, the yard I imagine outside, the steps outside the front door, the back door leading to the garage—is the house where I grew up. The room I am lying in is my bedroom in Canton, a large, south-facing space with three windows. As I come to consciousness, I have to deliberately resituate myself into the Cleveland Heights house I've lived in for over thirty years and into my present smaller bedroom, facing north, where I sleep with my husband. I have to deliberately reorient myself to these "new" surroundings. It's as though the default home in my mind is the house where I grew up.

East of my childhood home, about two city blocks away, ran a railroad track, and in the 1950s and 1960s, trains ran more frequently than they do now. During the day, when the train whistle blew, our neighbor dog Sarge, a big old collie, would light out for the train and try to chase it down. At night as I lay in my bed, conscious of my mom in the next room, aware of my dad downstairs, listening to my sisters breathing or turning in their beds, and Abbie twitching and murmuring in her private canine dreams, I would hear that train whistle from far in the distance growing nearer. It was a nighttime, haunting sound. And in the city where I now live, there's a railroad track somewhere in the distance, and sometimes, late at night, when I'm lying in the dark, I can hear the train whistle. When I hear it now, sleepless or on my way to sleep, it makes me feel mournful, but it also makes me feel at home.

Every now and then, when my dad was making some repair, he would send me down to the basement to search for a tool or piece of hardware that he recalled having used years before on his workbench. In all the years I knew him, he never went into the basement. He never went into our attic. After his downstairs bedroom was added, he never again went upstairs.

My dad's old workbench sat in a corner of our dim basement. On the left were makeshift shelves filled with baby-food jars holding screws and clamps and nails. On the right, more shelves held big cans of drying house paint. The workbench itself was covered with old tools and items whose purpose I never knew: bits of wood, screwdrivers, nuts and bolts, clamps, and other mysterious hardware. It had frozen in time at that vague moment in the past, the last time my dad had come downstairs. On the front of the bench was a vise that my father had made. I liked to play with it. I turned the big handle and moved the vise in and out so it would grasp something and hold it tight for gluing.

Sometimes he needed an artifact stored in our shed, a rickety building in our backyard that held more old tools, a couple of bikes, some old worn-out furniture. I would run outside and open the shabby wooden door, revealing hoes, saws, a huge cement roller once used to smooth down the lawn, rusty buckets, hoses, and shovels. But I remember best the faded green canvas awnings. I understood that they had once graced our home's upstairs windows, providing shade in the hot Ohio summers. They smelled musty, a smell that signified the past to me. Those awnings possessed a romance, and I longed to see how they looked on the front of our house. When I asked my mom about them, she responded sadly that they were of no use anymore.

So many things in our house were, in my time, of no use anymore. In our basement, fruits and vegetables canned by my mother filled a closet, untouched, ignored. These jars sat on those shelves all my life, never moved, never opened, never dusted. We threw them away when we sold the house, thirty years after my dad first became ill. Another corner of the basement held the deep freezer, empty during most of my childhood, except for big tubs of ice cream (of which Marge and I sometimes sneaked big spoonfuls) and for the occasional sides of beef my parents bought. I was given to understand, though, that it had once stored the wealth of my father's garden from the years before I could remember.

Even corners of our living area were like sealed-off museum displays. A large china cabinet in our dining room was filled with beautiful antique dishes we never used. The linen closet upstairs contained a dozen pairs of high-heeled shoes from the thirties and forties. In my lifetime, my mother suffered from corns and other foot ailments and wore big orthopedic shoes, of which she complained bitterly. I loved dressing up in her old fancy shoes, but I would have been more excited to see her wear them. The closet was filled with bottles and jars of desiccated ointments and soaps and lotions, in addition to the sheets and towels stuffed onto the shelves. I thought of this closet as a drugstore that could be raided for shoe polish, shoelaces, Vick's VapoRub, conditioners, shampoos, permanents, hair rollers and clips. Stuff sat in that closet for years and years. If you reached in far enough, you could find whatever you wanted.

In my dad's room rested the big parallel bars, unused except by me and my sisters. In addition to framing my hogan, they provided a perch from which I could talk with my dad when he was sick in bed. In his small bathroom, added when we built the addition, was a shower, rarely used. After he died, it stored vast supplies of toilet paper. For some reason, my mother always hoarded six or eight or twelve packages of toilet paper there, so much that my husband still jokes about it. My mom purchased all of these from the Cook Coffee man.

My mother had a whole stable of door-to-door salespeople. The Cook Coffee man sold her everything from toilet paper to dish cloths and knickknacks. I guess he sold coffee, too. The Fuller Brush man visited occasionally, and we had a Nickles Bakery guy and a milkman nicknamed Brownie. Over the years, a variety of Avon ladies stopped by periodically to show their wares. My mother bought cosmetics and perfumes for herself, which she rarely used, and for us as well. We each had our favorite scent: Sweet Honesty for me, Occur for Marge, and Topaz for Betsey.

These came in decorative bottles, and today, of course, many of them have become valuable. On a website for Avon collectibles, I find the term *fan rockers*. So those little bottles have a name. They are dated around 1962, which is just about right. Shaped like upside-down fans, they can literally rock from side to side on their curved bottoms. The sides have ridges, and narrow up to a point, topped by a gold plastic cap, with a little sash tied around it. The bottles came in small, neat boxes, and the color of the box indicated which scent it was.

When I was about eleven, I gave one of these bottles of Avon perfume to my mom. It was probably To a Wild Rose, which seemed an old-fashioned scent, appropriate for a mother. I can't remember now how I acquired it. I suppose it's possible I secretly bought it myself from the Avon lady. More likely, I selected it from one of my mother's three large dresser drawers filled with gifts she had received and never used, as well as items she had purchased and hadn't given to anyone. And never would. When she died, we sorted through those drawers and gave things away. I remember beautiful lacy slips and colorful nightgowns and robes. My mom's everyday slips were droopy and old, the straps fastened with safety pins. The pale pink flannel nightgowns she always wore had been washed so many times they were sheer (in fact, I'm just guessing they were originally flannel), hanging down in tatters, and she never wore a robe that I can remember. All those bright, clean, new items in her drawers went to Goodwill after she died.

Most likely, I picked out that perfume myself from her stash, because it made sense to my eleven-year-old mind to "shop" from those drawers. I wrapped it in some light blue paper and gave it to her for her birthday. Smiling slightly, she set it aside and opened other packages. When she came to the end, the blue box was still there.

"Why don't you open it?" I asked.

"I know what it is," she answered evenly. "I don't need to open it."

That made sense to me at the time. When it's your mother speaking to you, you make it make sense. It was like Santa Claus, who, we were told early on, did not exist. That's how we dealt with such things. These topics bore no relation to feelings, or sentiment, or "fun." They were in the area of fact. In fact, my mom did know what was in that box, because the size and shape were so familiar. What was the point of opening it?

Eventually the little blue-wrapped box made its way to her dusty dressing table, scattered with other neglected perfumes, lipsticks, and powders. I can picture it sitting on her dresser for years and years. It sat there, in fact, for about thirty years. Like all the rest, it was there when we were selling the house and cleaned out her room. As a teenager, I would occasionally ask her, partly joking, when she was planning to open it. She would repeat, impassively, that there was no need because she knew what was inside.

28

Finally, I just stopped asking.

I wasn't angry or disappointed. I was merely bewildered. It was a gift from her daughter that she never bothered to open. I never verbalized how odd this was. I have just always carried with me the vivid image of that box on the dresser.

Now, as an adult, I try to explain. I try to explain my mother.

I was driving to a restaurant recently with a friend of mine. She was putting on some Avon lipstick and told me, sheepishly, that she had an Avon lady, and we laughed about how retro that was. We got talking about Avon products, and I mentioned that old Avon bottles were collectible.

She knows a little about my mother, and so I recalled for the first time in many years that unopened gift. I had never told anyone about it before, never realizing it was a "story." Now, suddenly, I expected my account would automatically convey my mother's hoarding, insensitivity, and determined passivity. That gift, thirty years: a blatant symbol of strangeness. But my friend said, Oh, Kathy, she loved you so much. She wanted to keep it.

No, I said, it wasn't that.

But, she insisted, you were her favorite, weren't you? She must have cherished that present.

No. I could only say, No. It wasn't that. Suddenly I felt very impatient with my friend and very angry with my mother.

It's always like this. Where to begin? That box is not evidence that my mother loved me. No indication of "cherishing" at all, but rather of eccentricity and disconnection. It seems now a symptom of illness.

One night, during the time I was writing this chapter, I had the following dream. I was riding up a rickety wooden escalator to an attic. The surroundings were unfamiliar, but when I arrived at the attic, I knew it was my mother's, and I knew it was filled with her stuff. There were boxes packed with envelopes and documents bound with twine. I knew that this was a vast store of information about my mother—memorabilia, letters, legal papers—that I had

29

never seen before. I picked up boxes at random and looked inside at unfamiliar names and addresses. I continued to know, as you "know" in dreams, that this was my mother's attic and this was her stuff, but nothing I looked at made any sense, and I wasn't able to approach anything in an organized way. I randomly pulled letters out of piles, aware that I was disturbing whatever order was there. I could make no sense of what I was seeing. Finally, I decided to leave but couldn't find my way out. There were no doors, and the windows were locked, and anyway I was too far off the ground to jump out. At last, I got back in the makeshift contraption and figured out how to work it. As I left the attic, it seemed more and more as though the house really wasn't my mother's. The escalator led to a back door, and I walked around the outside of the old square brick house—completely unfamiliar to me—and it seemed it was not my mother's house after all.

She has remained a painful mystery to me, though the evidence lies all around. Her tattered nightgowns, her criticism, her emotional absence, and her stacks of old magazines in the kitchen were documents that I couldn't read. I have set my mind now to interpreting them all.

Drinking

My dad usually took a swig from a whisky bottle before dinner, sometimes two. Then he'd often down a beer or two in the evenings and have several on weekend afternoons while watching a ball game on TV. I grew to dread his drinking, because his personality changed subtly as he drank. His words slurred, his voice grew louder, and his jokes were not so funny. I felt embarrassed for him and imagined friends coming over (which was rare, anyway), worrying that they would see this sloppy guy instead of my articulate and witty dad.

When I was young, my mother made weekly trips to the grocery store and regular, if not quite weekly, trips to the liquor store. We'd journey from our suburban home to downtown Canton, an aberration from our usual routes to and from church and school. At Nicola's, a city wine shop, my mom would purchase a big bottle of Gallo port wine, which I have since learned is particularly potent, and a case of Iron City beer. The friendly clerks there recognized us, and a huge, silent, forbidding-looking man would carry the beer out to the car. Then we'd stop in at the state liquor store nearby and pick up a bottle of whisky for my dad.

Every evening Mom would sip her wine from a small glass as she watched TV. She, too, changed as she drank. She'd appear unfocused, and her speech became labored. She'd walk tipsily around the house and had trouble climbing the stairs. Sometimes in the morning she didn't recall conversations we'd had the night before.

One evening, we were leaving a PTA meeting at my grade school. My mom tripped and fell as we walked down the school drive. I don't think she had been drinking. But my friend Claudia's mom, helping her up, seemed embarrassed and apologetic for her. Claudia told me later that she had mentioned my mother's drinking wine every night to her parents, and I realized that Claudia's mom thought she was drunk. I was mortified and tried hard not to think about it.

My parents' drinking increased gradually over time, and so my older sisters, who went off to college and then married, were less aware of it than I. Then, after my father died, and my mother gradually stopped driving, she mostly stopped drinking as well, except for the occasional cocktail or glass of wine at a restaurant.

I was probably in my thirties before I first considered the possibility that my parents were problem drinkers. But I had always known that their drinking was a problem for me.

Church

I step inside our back door on a Sunday morning, and the smells of a rich breakfast fill my nose. Bacon and sausage are browning in the electric frying pan that sits on the kitchen table in front of my dad. He greets us there every Sunday when we return from church, with breakfast almost ready. All that's left to do is for my mother to toast the English muffins—loaded with butter—and for my dad to fry the eggs. They coordinate the timing so that the eggs don't overcook and the muffins don't burn. For most of my childhood, I was too persnickety to eat the eggs, but I loved watching them fry, and when I saw everyone else enjoying them, I wished I liked them, too.

Sometimes my sisters and I bicker, and my dad might say something about how we all just came from church, didn't we? My dad isn't Catholic. He was raised in the Methodist church and in other Protestant churches but isn't much of a believer, as far as I can tell. It doesn't seem to trouble him that the rest of us are Catholic. My maternal grandfather wasn't Catholic, either, and I note, as I get older, that I'm Catholic only because of a lone Catholic grandparent, my mom's mother, who came over on the boat from Ireland when she was about five. The other three grandparents and my dad were Protestants.

We have just come home from St. Paul Church in North Canton, an elegant old brick building in that pretty town. It has an ornate white marble altar and dark wood pews. A big old rectory with a front porch sits alongside, next to a dark red brick school and a separate convent on the green, well-manicured grounds. The sidewalks crisscross the lawn. St. Paul's School, where I attend Sunday school, has wooden desks with wrought-iron legs bolted to the floor and huge windows with shades. The nuns use long, hooked rods to pull them down. It's a more old-fashioned building than the public school I attend during the week. The nuns wear traditional black habits with wimples and tuck their handkerchiefs into their voluminous sleeves. They're formal and serious with us, but never mean. I remember one telling us that we are lucky to attend a public school, because by meeting so many non-Catholics we would learn that people who aren't Catholic can be good and admirable. Sometimes, she said, children in Catholic schools get the wrongheaded notion that only Catholics are good.

We often attend the 10:45 Mass, because we all like to sleep late. It's the high Mass, my favorite. A long procession comes down the aisle, led by Monsignor Steiger wearing an ornate brocade vestment. He swings a censer overflowing with aromatic smoke. The deep voices of the men's choir sing, *Asperges me, Domine, hyssopo et mundabor. Lavabis me, et super nivem dealbabor.* It doesn't matter that I don't know what they're saying. I love hearing their powerful voices pour down from the dark-wood choir loft above and behind us.

I don't mind Mass at all. I like looking around at all the people. I'm intrigued by the fathers sitting with their families, because I never see my own father in a suit and tie, standing and walking out in public with his family. I enjoy seeing everyone dressed up. I like the missals with their smooth ribbon bookmarks. I like trying to follow along with the Latin on the left-hand pages. I like the huge white marble altar.

But maybe the pleasantest part of Sunday is that fragrant greeting at home, the cheerful bacon smell of the only breakfast we eat together all week. It's about noon when we get back, and I'm always hungry. I like that my dad has breakfast ready for us.

One Saturday a month we go to Confession. I veer to the right when we enter the church, Mom goes left. I prefer the serious, bespectacled young associate, Father Rudnick. He has pale skin and black hair and a scholarly demeanor, and I have a little crush on him. Kneeling briefly to pray, I prepare by reading my blue pamphlet, "Examination of Conscience." It suggests dozens of sins, and I pick out a few. I can usually honestly confess that I fought with my sister or that I gossiped, but that doesn't seem like enough, so the rest I select arbitrarily. Did you lie? Did you cheat? Did you have impure thoughts? One of my favorites, unaccountably, is "I made fun of old people," and I use it almost every week, even though I am never even tempted to make fun of old people. Inside the dark confessional, Father Rudnick gently assigns me five Hail Mary's, which I recite to myself back outside in the pew.

My mother, on the other side of the church, confesses to the pastor, Monsignor Steiger. In his Sunday sermons, he rants against interfering mothers-in-law, calling them battleaxes, and against the edicts of Rome. He opposes the changes that Vatican II imposed, bellowing Sunday after Sunday, "They change things, and then they change the changes." He scares me, but my mother insists that he's mild-mannered and kind in the confessional, and when I finally screw up the courage to try him out, I find it to be true.

The mystery to me is what my mother confesses. I have never heard her apologize or admit to any fault. I always wonder what sins she confesses, and even now, I try to imagine what she whispered to the priest in the confessional.

When I am fourteen, the diocese abruptly changes our parish boundaries. Suddenly we are members of another church, called Little Flower, four miles away in another direction, in the tiny town of Middlebranch. Angry and incredulous, I want to resist. How can they take away our church? How can we suddenly "belong" somewhere else—no farewell, no ceremony, no fuss at all? I express my indignation, my sadness, hoping my mother will agree. But she merely shrugs, seemingly unfazed by the change. She has attended St. Paul's for twenty years. How can she *not* mind?

In retrospect, I see her nonchalance as consistent with her attitude about church. It was important enough for her to dutifully attend Mass on Sundays and holy days and go to confession frequently. We never attended daily Mass, however, and I grew up not knowing what a novena was or learning the Glorious Mysteries, like other cradle Catholics did. We never attended social activities at church and didn't pray together, except with my grandmother. We never read Scripture.

As I got older, I wondered why her faith provided no comfort to her. I wondered why she didn't pray or visit the priest to talk. I wondered why she made no friends at church. Attending Mass every Sunday was just something we did. When I went to high school and then to college, I lost interest in church. I still liked the music and was moved by the ritual, but the rest I could take or leave. I kept attending church on Sundays only to avoid my mom's criticism, and because I felt obligated to take her. Sometimes, I could even coax her into driving home, and that made me feel as if I had accomplished something.

Much later, after I had children of my own, and after I found church people I admired and liturgy that moved me, I found a tenuous niche in the Catholic Church. My faith gave me aspirations and hope, and the community gave me emotional and spiritual support. If my mother found those things in the Church, if she ever found solace in worship, faith, or prayer, I never witnessed it. The word she used most often to describe her connection to the Catholic Church was *duty*.

Sisters

Betsey was angry. It seemed to me that Betsey was often angry, but in this particular instance, I suppose she had good reason. She was searching in her closet for her white high-heeled shoes and found in one of them a tall, neat mound of talcum powder. Why, she wailed, would someone pour talcum powder in my shoe? Why, indeed?

Why did I do such a thing? At eight, I was old enough to know it was a bad thing to do, and more than a little odd. I remember my meditative mode, how much I enjoyed merely sneaking into Betsey's room. That day, I crept into her closet and saw the shoe, and then I saw the bath powder on her dresser, and it just seemed to me that they went together. The sweet-smelling stuff made such a satisfying soft delicate mountain sticking out of her shoe!

After all, I often thought, was it fair that she had her own room, when Marge and I had to share a room? Was it fair that she had a "new" room, built over our garage ten years earlier for the few years my dad's mother had lived with us? That she had a walk-in closet, with lots of shelves, and a window in the closet looking out over our driveway and the backyard? Though quite small, it always seemed to me more like an apartment than a kid's room.

None of these things was fair, so it seemed only right to trespass, as Marge and I occasionally did. And why not fill one of those pretty grown-up shoes with talcum powder? I didn't feel any conscious malice as I did so. I just felt like it would be fun, and it was.

For Betsey, though, younger sisters were a trial. She tolerated me pretty well most of the time, at worst being condescending. For example, I remember her commenting that it had probably been best, on November 22, 1963, to let "little kids" like me just stay in school after hearing about President Kennedy's assassination. I was furious, at twelve, to be called a little kid and to have it assumed that we would be unmoved by the president's death.

Where I was nearly beneath notice, Marge was a serious thorn in Betsey's side. Their sibling rivalry resulted in hair-pulling, knock-down fights. To me, Betsey was grown up, mature, and distant, and often in a bad mood. She was exotic. Eight years older than I, she went to high school. She wore bobby sox and saddle shoes. She sewed some of her own clothes. She carried a cool leather binder with a zipper and had yearbooks with her picture in them and wore a red Glenwood High School jacket.

Other than Betsey's distress, I don't remember any repercussions for my weird act of vandalism. I think my mother may have mildly reprimanded me, or asked me for an explanation. I didn't have one, and the subject was dropped. Betsey remained fascinating but unapproachable to me, until we were both grown up.

If Betsey seemed remote, Marge was a playmate, a mentor, and a torment. I spent more time with Marge than with anyone else. Sometimes, I was a pest to be rid of. She and her friend Trudy would suggest Hide and Seek, tell me to hide, and never come find me. If we played cowboys and Indians, or even when we played house, I was the first to die. Once they locked me and Trudy's brother Kurt in a dark fruit cellar for what seemed an eternity. Other times, it was just Marge and me—climbing trees, playing with the neighborhood dogs and Chuck Dill, walking to a neighbor's to ride horses, swimming at our neighborhood pool, or lying in our bedroom talking.

Marge was daring and rebellious. She adopted stray dogs and cats. She was late coming home. She occasionally raged at my parents. In high school, she cut classes a couple of times. I admired her and was intimidated by her and listened to her. My mother criticized Marge frequently, calling her irresponsible, and she often complained to me about Marge. I weighed what she said. I perceived, pretty early, that Marge was sometimes disrespectful, sometimes foolhardy, and that my mom was critical and severe when it came to Marge. I knew, deep down, that my mother should not be talking to me about my sister, but this became an enduring habit.

In 1962, Betsey failed my mother in a big way. Always an excellent, conscientious student, she flunked out of Western Reserve University. She had taken on a major in math, and it proved to be too much for her.

From my perspective as a ten-year-old, this was a shattering failure, because my mother treated it that way. Betsey had let everyone down, she had wasted thousands of dollars, and she had upset my mother's carefully laid plan.

My mother claimed to have deliberately had her children four years apart, so that there would be only one child in college at a time, and when one of us graduated, she could help financially with the next. When Betsey foiled the plan, my mother became enraged. As the youngest child, the one most often at home, I heard about Betsey's betrayal every day. I never once heard, or wondered about, Betsey's feelings on the matter.

She behaved like a trooper. She stayed out of school the required semester and then returned to Reserve, where she eventually earned a degree in English. After her graduation in 1965, she got a job and an apartment in Cleveland, an hour away from us, and made plans to marry her boyfriend Art.

This amounted to another betrayal, another crisis. More tears and upset. What about the plan? Betsey had agreed, my mother constantly told me, to come back home and pay my parents back for college. Why would a young single girl live in an apartment by herself? What must she be doing there with her boyfriend? Why would she pay rent to strangers instead of helping her parents?

In the meantime, another crisis ensued. My sister Marge flunked out of Ohio State, overwhelmed by a devastating break-up with a boyfriend. Rewind: mother crying, ranting, bewailing her daughters' failures. Marge compounded this second betrayal by immediately getting an apartment with friends in Columbus instead of moving back home. I witnessed the constant tears, heard the scathing criticism, and felt the crushing disappointment. I heard it over and over. Marge had further spoiled my mother's plan.

It got worse. Marge became pregnant in 1968 with a new boyfriend and married him. Although my mother grew fond of Marge's daughter, Stephanie, and although in time Marge also finished college and later earned graduate degrees in both law and library science, nothing healed the wounds she had inflicted.

Twenty years later, I asked Betsey about "the plan." Did you agree, I asked, to move back home and pay rent to help with Marge's and my tuition? Betsey looked at me blankly. "This is the first I've heard of that," she said. "I thought Mom just didn't like Art."

All the time my mother was telling me about Betsey's perfidy, she had never raised the subject with Betsey. She thought Betsey just should have known. I took a lesson from my mother's anger and recriminations. When it came time for me to go to college, I stayed home. I enrolled at our local campus of Kent State University, because I was afraid that if I went away to school like my sisters, I would also flunk out. I knew all too well how my mother would react if I failed like my sisters. I didn't want her to talk about me the same way she talked about them.

All during these painful times, my dad may have worried about his daughters' choices but was reconciled to them. I have a few amusing letters that he wrote to Marge after she'd gotten an apartment and a waitressing job in Columbus, warning her how difficult waiting tables was going to be. "So you are now a waitress," he wrote. "You are about to learn more in two weeks than you ever learned before in your life." He reminded her that when he waited table at a fraternity at Ohio State, if he spilled coffee in the saucer, he had to return to the kitchen and "try another run." Concerned about Marge's future, he advised her that working would add "self-imposed hurdles in the education race." Then he added reasonably, "Howsomever, it is your choice," and ended on this light note: "Don't let any handsome boys switch vegetables on the menu, and always push the blue-plate special. Beware of big tippers." That any such affectionate advice might come from my mother is unimaginable to me. To my mother, Marge's decisions were calamitous and cruel.

I've never known how my dad regarded my mother's hysterical reactions. I suspect that he took the responsibility on himself. I think he took everything on himself. If he hadn't gotten sick, if he had been able to be a better husband, my mother would be happy.

Loss

I'm twelve years old. I enter the kitchen, approaching my dad from behind, already talking to him. He shushes me. He gestures to the radio, which is always on and always set to Canton's WHBC, and listens to the quiet folk song playing there for a minute or two. I have heard the song before, but it made no impression. It is Peter, Paul, and Mary singing "Blowin' in the Wind." When it ends, he says to me, in amazed appreciation, "That song is about civil rights."

Seven years later—in May of 1970—I walk into the kitchen again, and my dad sits in the same spot, leaning intently toward the radio. National Guardsmen have killed four students at Kent State University. I had already heard the news and, even though I am a freshman at a KSU branch campus, I had numbly filed the incident away as another act of violence, like the assassinations of Robert Kennedy and Martin Luther King Jr. But my dad looks worried. He shakes his head and says, "This is bad. This is very bad."

He was ahead of me in most matters.

In the fall of 1970, my dad began to have trouble swallowing. When he went to the doctor, he was told he had a tumor in his throat. I was a freshman in college, living at home. He went for weekly radiation treatments, transported in a local funeral home's ambulance. These trips wore him out, and he developed a painful rash on his neck and chest, but the radiation worked, and the tumor disappeared.

The following spring, he developed new symptoms. He lost his appetite and coughed up a rheumy phlegm. His doctor, the same physician who had misdiagnosed him in 1953, told him he had tuberculosis, based on a lab test.

He stayed in a quarantined room in the hospital taking antibiotics. When we visited him, we had to wear face masks and papery yellow robes. The antibiotics didn't work, and he continued to get sicker.

Finally, one day when my mom and I visited him, he told us that the doctor had visited that morning and apologized. The lab had made a mistake, and there was no TB. In fact, the cancer had returned and spread to the rest of his body, including his liver. I remember how intensely he watched us as he spoke. My mother responded vaguely that it was good he didn't have TB. My father looked at her sternly and raised his voice. "Eleanore, they can treat TB," he said.

When we left that room, I felt that my father and I were the only people who understood that he had a terminal illness. My mother seemed uncomprehending, and we never spoke about it. By this time, both my sisters had married. Marge lived in town, and Betsey lived outside of Cleveland. Maybe someone told them that the cancer was back, but it wasn't me. I couldn't speak of it. It was too horrible, and the words stuck in my throat. I felt that it was a betrayal of my father to say it out loud. Acknowledging it would make it real. He was going to die, and I was the only one aside from the doctors, who knew.

My father came home from the hospital and stayed in bed. A visiting nurse—gracious, good-humored, and kind—stopped by daily to care for him. I continued to attend my college classes and spent time in his room with him, trying to make normal conversation. Sometimes, I urged my dad to eat, and he would explain, peevishly, that he really couldn't. I remember sitting perched on his parallel bars, watching him lying in his bed and looking out the window.

Betsey visited, and I felt impatient with her for seeming not to understand what was happening. She didn't go into his room right away and didn't seem to comprehend his dire situation. Somehow, the idea of broaching the subject with her didn't occur to me. She left not knowing he was dying, and it wasn't until later that I blamed myself for not communicating with her. My mother remained oblivious, and I felt overwhelmed with the reality that my father would die. I lived in a dark shadow of fear and silence.

Finally one afternoon at the end of April, I heard the nurse say to my dad, "Martin, I think it's time you went back to the hospital." He calmly assented. She got on the phone to the doctor, and I picked up the receiver upstairs and listened in.

She said something about his liver and about metastasis and carcinoma, the first time I had ever heard those words. The doctor said he knew and that, yes, it was probably time. She said, "I like Martin." He answered, "I do, too."

When I came downstairs, ready to go to school, the nurse was calling the ambulance and preparing my dad for the hospital. I asked him if he wanted me to skip school and go with him. He emphatically said, "No, no. You go to school."

So I did. Later in the day, I looked up those unfamiliar cancer words and confirmed what I already knew.

When I got home, my mother and I decided for some reason not to visit my father. I have no idea now what we could have been thinking, but I called him and told him we weren't coming in. He hesitated and then said it was okay.

I'm pretty sure I called my sister Marge to tell her Dad was back in the hospital, but I'm not sure about Betsey, and I'm not sure about his sister, my aunt Betty. An old friend from the newspaper had been planning to visit him at home, and my mother called him to say that my dad was returning to the hospital.

The next day was a Saturday, and my mother and I went in to the hospital. My dad was mostly conscious, but not entirely coherent. He asked me to readjust his pillows, and, though I tried, I felt that I wasn't making him comfortable. He kept asking about his IV and seemed to think it wasn't working properly, and I tried to reassure him. Then he gestured to his drawer and insisted that my mother and I read a letter from his newspaper friend Mr. Mansell.

It said,

My visit scheduled for this afternoon will have to be postponed. I am writing this note, in the hope it will take the place of my presence at a time of big trouble for an old correspondent.

I am thinking of all the Letters from Max and the relatively few letters that went to Max. Just a few days ago, someone asked me about Max, and for the umpteenth time I tried to make a cogent answer.

Max, I explained, was someone special—an associate on the newspaper staff who had been blessed with a screwball mentality and cursed with a physical injury that had confined him to a bed and a wheelchair. I went on to explain, as I have done so many times over the years, that my friend Max had been a revelation to all of us because he had reached down inside himself and found resources of courage and resiliency that must have surprised him. Most certainly they astounded all of us who knew him, because we were sure in our minds that if the same thing had happened to us we would have been destroyed.

As the years went by, our compassion for a friend who had endured a tough break gradually was transmuted into admiration for the manner in which he had endured it. At this point in my exposition I always made the same summation: My friend Max has been a great and good example for all of us.

You are having big trouble. You know it. We all know it. In our various ways and with varying measures of success, all of us are trying to let you know how concerned we are.

My way—the best way I know—is to return one letter from me to you, in exchange for a delightful correspondence that went on for many years--the Letters from Max. Fact is, the correspondence was going on long before it became public, and it went on after it ceased to be shared with outsiders. I valued it beyond price.

I had intended to tell you about it this afternoon at your house. I am telling you about it in this note instead.

With all my good wishes, Darrel

My mother read the letter without reacting and handed it to me. As I read, I felt a profound relief that someone besides me had recognized what was happening. I was glad that my dad had been communicating with his friends about his illness and grateful that someone had acknowledged his "big trouble" to him. He looked intently at me and said, "Did you read it?" I nodded, afraid I was going to cry; for some reason that seemed like the worst possible thing I could do. Finally we said goodbye. At the door I looked back and said, "Bye, Dad." He said goodbye again.

When we got home, I went out to the shed in our backyard filled with old tools and straw and cried violently, alone.

Just before dawn, we were awakened by a call from the hospital. The nurse told me my father's condition had changed and we should come to the hospital. My mother and I dressed and drove in the eerie half-light to the hospital. The nurses told us in the hall that my father had died. We entered his room, and he lay on his back, his face gray, and his mouth gaping open. My mother stood shaking her head. She said, "When they called, I thought maybe he'd taken a turn for the better. I thought we'd come in and find him better."

Although I knew that my mother had seemed oblivious, I was stunned that she could have imagined a sudden recovery. Before we left, I took Darrel Mansell's letter from the drawer and kept it safe.

We drove home. It was too early to call anyone, so we sat in the kitchen waiting for a few hours. We drank coffee. No hugs, no touching, no commiseration. I cried continuously, and my mother looked impassively at me across the table. Occasionally she would say, "Poor Kathy." A few hours later, I went to the phone and called my sisters and my dad's sister. I don't recall my mother contacting anyone.

Sometimes, then and later, she would say that she felt the loss too deeply to cry. I could understand the lack of tears, I guess, but not the absence of any emotion at all. She once told Betsey that she had cried all her tears twenty years before when my father had first gotten sick. Now, she showed no outward signs of grieving, but a few weeks after my dad's death, she became so ill that Betsey came to stay with us to help nurse her back to health.

It took me many years to get past my father's death. Wise and funny and strong, he was the most important person in my life. I missed him very much.

He had left me alone with my mother. "I miss him a lot," I wrote in my journal, "when Mom begins to drive me crazy. He used to be the only relief, and I used to wonder how I could even live without him to provide a human being to talk to. I never wrote about her much before, maybe because I had Dad to help me live with her, to compensate for her. I'm afraid it's a very selfish way to miss Dad."

The most painful part of my grieving, though, was my own failure. I had failed to tell him how much I loved him. I failed him utterly. I hadn't told my sisters or my aunt what was happening and failed them, too. I was shut up, dumbstruck, silenced by terror at the thought of my dad's dying. I did everything wrong at a time when doing what's right was so important, when being deliberate and thoughtful and conscious would have counted for something.

When I try to forgive myself, I ponder that time of numb silence, during my father's illness and after his death. I recall sitting at the kitchen table, trying to absorb the fact that my father was dead, watching my mother's dispassionate face.

Falling from Grace

After a few dates with a young man I'll call John M., my first real boyfriend, I told my mother he was divorced. I remember feeling confidently mature in telling her this, thinking it wise to just get it out in the open. We were Catholics, but liberal Catholics. I don't remember hearing my parents say anything against divorce. My mother's best friend from college was divorced, and my mother had never disparaged her or any other divorced people. She revered Adlai Stevenson, after all, who was divorced.

So, I felt blindsided when, a few days after my revelation, my mother confronted me. She was angry, worried, and hurt. What could I be thinking? How could I possibly do such a thing? What was wrong with me? What had happened to my morals?

My sisters had had their crises with our mother. By her lights, they had betrayed her by failing in college, moving away, getting pregnant, and getting married. Their college degrees and other accomplishments, their jobs, their visits with their kids made no difference. My mother could be pleasant, but then, in the middle of an ordinary conversation, she would remind them of her disappointment.

This was how I fell from grace in my mother's eyes. Any mother, of course, might worry about her twenty-one-year-old's first boyfriend. John was four years older than I and had two kids. How could any mother, especially a Catholic mother, not be concerned?

My mother wasn't merely concerned. My mother wept and pleaded and shouted. At times, she refused to speak to me. She told me she considered suicide. I was ruining my reputation. All our relatives, she said, would be ashamed of me.

John M., a sweet-souled, honest fellow, imagined that if he could just talk to my mother, she'd see that he wasn't such a bad sort. Several times, he arranged to stop by our house while I was away at school, to talk things over with my mom. Each time, John would say things went well, and, in the immediate aftermath, my mother would admit that he wasn't so bad.

Then, a little later, the story would change. I would come upon her crying or walk into the kitchen and feel her glare. Now, it seemed, John had said dreadful things. Men like him could have sex with girls like me, there were no rules anymore, and she was behind the times. Suddenly furious, my mother called him a snake.

I nearly laughed. What guy would tell his girlfriend's mother that he could have sex with anyone he liked? Does such a stupid man exist? When I relayed my mom's version of things to John, he shook his head. He might have said that times had changed, meaning that people were more accepting of divorce than they used to be. My mother could twist an innocent remark like that into insidious depravity.

All conversations about John degenerated into my mother's weeping and shouting. I wasn't decent, she would say. My father would be ashamed of me. My relationship was sordid. She called me a hypocrite, because I continued to act nice on the outside, while I was so dirty on the inside. On her wedding anniversary, she said that because of me she wished she'd never gotten married. She seemed so irrationally overwrought that I almost smiled, but at the same time her desperation frightened me. I tried to understand why she was so unreasonable, so unwilling to listen. I hated lying to her about seeing John, but I couldn't imagine what else to do. If I broke up with him to please her, I would only resent her.

It gradually dawned on me that she had no life outside of me. Why don't you think about other things? I would ask. Why is it all about me? These questions offended her because I was minimizing the tremendous wound I had caused. I felt trapped. She had no interests, no activities, no friends, no hobbies. I'd never realized before how focused on me she was. She said I used to be perfect, and it mystified me: she'd never expressed any particular appreciation before. If anything, she usually had been uncommunicative or even disapproving, but now I was given to understand that we had been devoted and close and loving. And I was throwing away our entire relationship for this snake.

More than once she said she was sure he had raped me.

My journals of the time include descriptions of a few reasonable conversations, as well. Sometimes she'd acknowledge that I needed to make my own decisions. She would say she didn't want to be bossy. I would think things were better, until the next explosion.

One afternoon I was talking to John M. on the upstairs phone, very quietly, hoping that my mother wouldn't hear. Although

I was in my twenties by now, away at graduate school much of the time, I still found it necessary to sneak around the house to avoid upsetting her. When I came downstairs, I could see from the expression on her face that she had heard me. She sat stiffly in her customary place at the kitchen table. Her hand clutched a knife. As I approached, she raised the knife and shrieked, "Slut! You slut!"

Our arguments went on for over two years while I continued to see John M. After I broke up with him and began dating the man I eventually married, the recriminations didn't end. Until she died, twenty years later, when I was happily married with two children, she would still bring up that betrayal. I was never again the good person she had once thought I was.

The Glance in the Hallway

A story of another dog.

Abbie entered the family soon after Snap died, when I was eight and Marge, animal lover extraordinaire, was twelve. Abbie was the dog of my childhood, the dog that lasted, the dog of my life until my adult family acquired a dog. A smallish black-and-white cocker mix, Abbie was an undemanding, intelligent dog. In her prime, her chief eccentricity was that she climbed trees.

A giant willow tree stood near the street in our front yard. Its trunk's circumference was, I'm guessing, about fifteen feet. The lowest branches grew out just over our heads, maybe five feet up, so climbing the tree required getting a purchase on the trunk's rough black bark with our feet as far up as possible, and then heaving ourselves vertically to grab those massive branches with our hands. When we'd pulled ourselves up, we had a comfortable seat, enclosed in the dark, leafy grandeur of that tree.

I can't remember when she learned to climb up after us, but I imagine Abbie felt pretty lonely, left at the bottom. She must have gazed up dolefully at her two favorite people, and whined and paced. At some point, Marge must have begun coaxing her. "Ab-

47

bie!" she'd call, patting her thighs and clapping, and Abbie would make a run up the trunk, and then slide back onto the soft grass.

Eventually, Abbie deduced the physics of the matter. She'd back up a few feet and make a run for it. Sometimes, she wouldn't have enough momentum and would slip down on the lawn. She'd keep backing up—there was no stopping her—until she had left enough distance between her and the tree to get a bona fide running start. Then she would literally run up the side of the tree, and we would grab her—her heart racing—into our arms. She'd sit on our laps, up in the willow, surveying our spacious front yard and the street below. At last, when we'd all gotten bored or hungry (Abbie was always hungry), we'd give her a nudge, and she'd leap more or less gracefully down to the ground.

The maple tree in the corner of the front yard was actually a much better climbing tree both for us and for Abbie. A big branch grew off to one side, about three feet up, making a huge V, just the right height to reach with your foot. Abbie could easily leap up this far. Another giant branch hung almost over the street, comfortable and polished from our sitting. These properties made for easy climbing. Abbie would run out of the house in front of us and wait by the tree. We'd climb up, and she would jump after us. She could sit on the branch or in our laps, leaning against us with our arms around her, in that comfortable position our dogs so often assume with us. I can feel her now, warm and soft and panting. Finally, of course, Marge grew up and grew beyond tree-climbing and left it to me for a few more years. All alone, with or without Abbie, I could take a book or a snack up in that tree and relax for a long time.

When I was a child, I found it miraculous, funny, and wonderful that our dog climbed trees. Everyone knew that cats climb trees, but who had ever heard of a tree-climbing dog? It probably wasn't so remarkable, although I must say that the neighbor dogs who always hung out in our yard, the collie mixes Laddie and Sarge, never attempted a climb. They were content to loll around in the grass, when they weren't chasing cars.

I often needed to get out of sight, to escape from complicated, emotional adult goings-on inside our house. Abbie and the trees provided a haven: cool shade, a breeze rustling the leaves, and a sweet, uncomplicated dog.

At the time of this story, though, tree-climbing was behind her. Abbie had somehow become fifteen or sixteen years old. It was three years after my father's death. I would soon be returning to graduate school at Kent State's main campus after summer break at home, again abandoning my dog to the ministrations of my mother, who had never wanted the dog (as she always repeated). Her interactions with Abbie consisted of a hissed "Pest!" when the dog came into view. It wasn't fair—I felt this keenly—to leave my mother with a dog that belonged to my sister and me. And now Abbie, a pet my mother never wanted, was elderly and disabled.

Her walking was stiff; it seemed to hurt her to move. She suffered from an allergy that inflamed her eyes, for which she required eye drops. She was pretty much blind. When the furniture was in its accustomed place, she was okay, but when the desk chair in the living room was pulled out, she would walk into it.

Worse, she was incontinent. Or, at least, she couldn't make it to the door in time, and so she dribbled on her way to the front door. If my mother, none too spry herself, could somehow let her out in time, how would Abbie find her way back into the house? Was it fair to expect my mother to keep her eye on the dog all day?

I must have mulled over the options for a period of time, but now I don't remember when the idea of putting Abbie down occurred to me. I don't know if I consulted Marge, but suddenly it seemed clear to me. That was the only thing to do. And I felt a great pressure. I had to go back to school. Marge lived in an upstairs apartment with a baby and with a husband who didn't like dogs. I lived in a dorm, and I couldn't take Abbie with me, and I couldn't leave her for my mom to care for.

I told Mom that I was thinking of putting Abbie to sleep. No doubt I hoped she'd say, "No need for that! I can take care of her for awhile longer!" At the same time, it was inconceivable that she would say such a thing.

She responded noncommittally but with a very, very slight assent. As I recall, it was more or less a shrug, meaning do what you have to do. I called Marge, who understood, and agreed that it was probably time. She asked me if I wanted her to accompany me to the vet. At that time, unaware of my own needs, I thought it was weak to ask for help and said no.

I called the vet. I drove there. I petted the dog as I drove, hardly able to think about what I was about to do. I opened the car door and lifted her out and walked into the waiting room. I remember people sitting there with dogs and cats that were merely sick and about to be treated. The girl at the counter greeted me. Unable to speak, about to burst into tears, I handed Abbie over to her. The girl looked at me empathetically and asked me if I wanted to stay. I shook my head, wordlessly. I was about to cry, and I couldn't allow myself to cry in front of her and all those people in the waiting room.

I drove home weeping. Immediately, I wished I had stayed at the vet's with the dog and hated myself for abandoning her there. When I got home, I took the vacuum sweeper to my bedroom and violently swept the dog hair from the carpet, crying. This loss seemed to bring up other losses. I dimly realized that I was crying for my father as much as for my dog. I cried so hard that my chest hurt, and I remember thinking that maybe this is why people say their hearts are breaking.

I looked up and saw my mother standing in the hallway. She was watching me, as I was vacuuming and crying. Our eyes met. Then she looked away and walked down the hall. During whatever time passed before I left for school, we didn't speak about the dog, about my feelings, about my taking the dog to the vet alone, about what happened there, about my crying in my room. We talked of none of it.

People suffer debilitating illnesses and the deaths of spouses and children. The death of pets is sad and painful but not comparable to these other losses. The reason for this story is not so much the death of Abbie. It is the mystery of that glance in the hallway. My mother saw me. She paused. She said nothing. Then she turned away.

Abandonment

"It's too bad he's named John. Those other two Johns were disasters."

During the time I was falling in love with my husband—another John, as it happens--I was ending the relationship that had so offended my mother. One would imagine she'd feel relieved, but not so. Instead, she hated John's name. She connected it, of course, with my divorced boyfriend, but she also connected it with the first name of Marge's now ex-husband, even though he was called by his middle name, Craig. My mother often made far-fetched connections between names or dates, and it drove me crazy. It seemed she was trying so hard to make things worse. She seemed perversely inclined to put the worst construction on things. It was as though she enjoyed being unhappy. She implied that I should break up with John merely because his first name disturbed her so.

She complained that we stayed out too late. John, a film buff, would usually take me to the movies, and she would say scornfully, "Hasn't he seen all the movies yet?" She told me that he gave her "bad vibes." When we were invited to Marge's house for a family event, she didn't want to go because he would be there. When she went anyway, she admitted he seemed nice and added that maybe she should warn him about me. "You're a bad girl," she said. "You used to be so good but now you're a bad girl. Maybe *he* should watch out for *you*."

She said, "All three of my daughters are losers."

We had one long talk in which I tried very hard to understand just what she didn't like about John. I could concede that the other boyfriend had his problems, from her point of view: he was divorced and older and had two kids. This new John, though, would seem like a parent's dream. He was my age. His very nice family owned a successful business. A Methodist, like my dad, he even taught Sunday school at his family's church. He had a college degree and a steady job. A teetotaler, he had never had a drink and, product of the sixties though he was, had never smoked marijuana. He was clean and pleasant and polite. What's not to like? I asked.

After vague criticisms, after recalling the hurt I'd caused her with the accursed boyfriend ("I haven't gotten over that. I just can't trust you anymore"), saying over and over that she didn't trust me and she didn't trust John, she finally broke down crying, so violently I had trouble understanding her words. But I recorded in my journal something like this: she was terrified someone would take me away from her. She would suspect and distrust and dislike anyone who might take me away. Her breaking down frightened me. I didn't know how to comfort her.

After a couple of years of dating, John and I decided to get married. My mom, of course, took no part in the planning. I went by myself to a Canton shop called The Parisian to pick out the off-white, street-length dress I would wear at my wedding. I hesitantly asked if she wanted to pay for anything, bracing myself for the scornful lecture I knew would follow. After the diatribe, she agreed to contribute something. When my future sister-in-law called to invite her to a wedding shower, she accepted, but only after unloading about how unhappy she was.

When we first revealed our marriage plans to our parents, I wrote in my journal, "Mother reacted badly, but not too badly." Then I explained what "not too badly" meant. She told me that she would never get over her disappointment in me. She repeated that my father would be ashamed of me. She said that every time she looked at my husband she would remember how much I had hurt her.

In the Kitchen

My mother sits in the kitchen. After my marriage, when I come to visit, she is facing the window that looks out into the backyard, where my father once had a garden. She sits eight feet or so from the window, the entire length of the kitchen table. At the end of the table rests a small portable TV, which my mother watches instead of looking out the window. Between her and the

TV lie piles of mail and magazines. The mail includes bills and bank statements, solicitations for donations, and junk mail.

The magazines merit their own paragraph. My mother subscribes to *The New Republic, Commonweal, Time, Harper's, Good Housekeeping, Atlantic Monthly, Saturday Review, TV Guide,* and *The New Yorker.* She also gets *The Repository,* and a few days worth of these always clutter the table as well. Magazines lie stacked on the kitchen floor. Piles of *Good Housekeeping* fill the corners, along with knickknacks and stacks of old mail.

Either the TV or the radio on the shelf beside her is always on. Sometimes a magazine lies open before her. She greets me pleasantly and says she's glad to see me. Occasionally, she has clipped articles from the paper to show me. They sometimes concern people my sisters or I knew in school, although she often confuses my friends with those of my sisters. Frequently, the clippings contain an admonition or chastisement—an Ann Landers column about preserving your virginity or some such thing.

When I was younger, my mother got some work done. She washed and ironed our clothes and cooked our meals, packed our lunches, washed dishes, and drove us here and there. Her household tasks generally did not include picking up, dusting, vacuuming, or heavier cleaning. She did do some of those things, but so infrequently that our messy house always embarrassed me. I could have taken on these chores myself, but I didn't think of it when I was very young, or I found them overwhelming. As I got older, I did do many of them, but felt disheartened that, far from thanking me, my mother ignored my efforts or complained of something being lost or out of place. Once when I had washed the kitchen floor—unwashed for many years—she asked me, "It wasn't so dirty, was it?" She seemed offended that I had presumed to take over.

At least when we were younger, she navigated a little more of the house. She slept upstairs and sat in the living room to watch TV. We have snapshots of her outside, of course, though she didn't play with us or go for walks. In her later years, after my father's death, she wore a path from the downstairs bedroom into which she had moved, to her kitchen chair, and back to the bedroom.

Most days, that was as far as she moved in a day.

My mother's activities diminished as soon as her daughters started driving. When we were all married and had moved out of the house, they largely ceased. She cooked a little for herself and washed her dishes but did no other cleaning. The last few years she was in the house, before she broke her hip and moved into a nursing home, I hired a cleaning lady who kept up the house and did the laundry.

In the mid-seventies, we hired my high-school friend Bob to paint the inside of my mother's house. He came every day and talked to my mom in the kitchen and went about his work. I was embarrassed that he saw our house and how my mother lived. He said, "Kathy, she doesn't do anything. She reads a lot of magazines, but nothing else. Why don't you do something? Don't you ever take her out?"

Well, she would go to Mass with me on Sundays. On birthdays and some other holidays, she went out to dinner. She visited the doctor and dentist. I cajoled her, over and over, to come to the grocery store with me, come out to lunch, come out, come out. She would shake her head and say no. When I asked why, she would say she didn't feel like it or wasn't feeling well. Most often, she'd just dodge the question.

She sleeps late most days. If I arrive around 11:00 a.m., or 2:00 p.m., in late afternoon or early evening, anytime of day, I know where to find her. She is sitting in the kitchen, sometimes just looking at the air.

Part II: Connecting the Dots

. . . something in my head clicked. It was a mechanical sensation, like one gear fitting into another. And then it was as if a small amount of pressure were relieved, a blister popped. Because now I had a name for what it was about my father that had always puzzled me, always been on the tip of my tongue and yet impossible to quite say. Before, I'd explained to myself that he was missing something. Or there was something off about him. But now I had the word for it.

Augusten Burroughs, *The Wolf at the Table*

Connections

It gives their confusing and contradictory childhood experience a name, an explanation, and most importantly, validation.

Kimberlee Roth, *Surviving a Borderline Parent*

At this point, I can no longer keep my memories in chronological order. I look back now, as an adult, and memories of my mother have organized themselves around mental illness, around the symptoms of borderline personality disorder. I have read, and read, and read about this disease. I have talked to my friend Nancy, who has received a borderline diagnosis (among other things) and who has become like a shaman, leading me to my mother in a dark underworld. As Nancy has gradually improved, her articulate descriptions of how she's feeling and how she used to feel and why she feels as she does have revealed my mother to me.

The connection came to me in a single moment. I had been learning a lot about BPD in my efforts to understand Nancy. Then one ordinary day, driving home from running errands, I was pondering yet again those long-ago bitter arguments with my mother. She repeated obsessively that I had always been perfect, but that I had completely changed. I was going to hell, I had injured her irreparably, and she would never be able to trust me. I drove along, musing once again—what did she mean by saying I'd been "perfect," why was I suddenly so awful, how she could have said such hurtful things, and how could I, a naïve twenty-year-old, have hurt her so badly?

BPD's most familiar symptom popped into my head: in the professional jargon, "extremes of idealization and devaluation." In other words, a person with BPD regards you as a saint one day and as a demon the next. It seemed like a textbook case. One day I was perfect, and the next I was horrible. It was an epiphany.

By now, I had committed the whole list of symptoms to memory in my efforts to understand my friend. Each one popped up in my mind. Avoiding abandonment? Yes, an obsession of my mother's. My sisters and I had even articulated that one.

Impulsivity? Maybe. My mother hoarded her money but occasionally splurged on odd purchases from the door-to-door salesmen who visited her. She suddenly had our decrepit kitchen redone without telling us, and sold her mother's china to a con artist, discarding these family heirlooms without consulting her daughters. She hung on to junk mail and old magazines for years but, after my father died, tossed away (unforgivably, to me) his correspondence. Some of my mother's behavior could surely be construed as impulsive.

She never tried suicide, but at the lowest points in our relationship, she told me she was considering it.

Mood swings and inappropriate intense anger? Yes, definitely yes.

Unstable relationships? Black and white thinking? An amorphous sense of self? All yes.

I didn't know if my mother felt empty inside. But suddenly it seemed quite plausible that she did.

When I arrived home, I grabbed the printout of these symptoms lying on my desk and called my sister Marge at work. "I'm going to read you a list," I said. "Tell me who it reminds you of."

I read the list of symptoms, and without hesitation, Marge said, "Mom."

A therapist would say my mom had an unstable affect. In my reading, I run across the term *inhibited grieving*. This line comes from A.J. Mahari, a BPD sufferer: "You cannot grieve what your defenses will not allow you to feel." My mother showed no outward signs of mourning, but instead may have manifested her grief in physical illness. People with BPD tend to fear feeling out of control and so tamp down their emotions or channel them in unhealthy directions. The more I read about BPD, the more it seemed my mother was finally being explained to me.

All of the BPD symptoms, taken individually, can seem like normal human behavior. We all fear abandonment. We all sometimes think in black and white. We often may act impulsively and experience mood swings. We may blame ourselves or others for our feelings. All of these are normal human reactions. BPD, like other mental illnesses, is an exaggeration of the normal. We all get depressed, for example, but we do not all suffer from depression—a ghastly, long-term affliction that interferes with a person's ability to sleep, work, and interact with others. Depression affects not only the sufferer, but the people who love the sufferer. So it is with BPD. It's a syndrome, a weird constellation of symptoms that hinder the sufferer's relationships and make her unhappy, angry, even self-destructive. Because it's a disorder of the emotions and relationships, it has an especially profound effect on family members and friends.

I have spent much of my life trying to figure out my mother. I have tried to understand our relationship and to forgive her. I have tried to forgive myself for hurting her. My mother died in 1995, and I still wrestle with questions I have about her. I'm still bitter about things she said to me. Every Lent, I ponder forgiveness and try to understand why she behaved as she did. Learning about a real mental illness—a chaotic and unpredictable one—is helping me, at last, to come to terms with my mom's inexplicable and wounding behavior. Now the memories coalesce around symptoms. Now my memories have a context.

I was not an abused child. I wasn't beaten or seriously neglected. In some ways, I was happy. I was fond of my two sisters, loved my mother, and admired and loved my father. But there was a pall over our household. My oldest sister Betsey once called it a "cloud of gloom." My mother, though sometimes superficially cheerful, was deeply unhappy. She expressed her unhappiness in ways that hurt all of us.

Dysphoria

The intensity of the pain and the amount of time suffering pain reported by borderline patients proves, by itself, easily capable of discriminating patients with BPD from those without . . . The results underscore that this disorder involves a terrible way to experience life.

John P. Gunderson, *Borderline Personality Disorder: A Clinical*

Guide

One Sunday morning, not long after my dad's death, Aunt Betty, my dad's sister, called to say that she and Uncle Rudy were coming to visit. This was the routine: every few months they'd call in the morning and then drive down to Canton from their home in Gates Mills, a Cleveland suburb. The phone call would give us about an hour to straighten up the house. We'd rush around removing junk from the couch, clearing clutter from tables and desks, and quickly dusting if there was time. After Dad died, my aunt and uncle continued these visits, and this was one of those days.

Betty and Rudy were rich. A chemist for a Cleveland oil company, Rudy had invested well. He was the only person I've ever known to call his broker daily to check his stock portfolio. Until he became a rabid environmentalist in the late seventies, he always drove a big new Buick. He and Betty traveled a lot and took home movies of their trips. I remember Rudy setting up his cumbersome 16 mm. projector on a card table in our living room and showing his movies, which consisted mostly of blooming cacti and unusual birds. He would narrate as the film unspooled, forgetting the names of about half of the species, while Betty shouted out additions and corrections. We girls were fond of Betty and Rudy, and they were also fond of us. Mom and Betty had been friends in college—Betty introduced my parents—but my mother resented their wealth. She would always remind us that Rudy had started out poor. When he was unemployed during the Depression, she said, Betty had to support them both by teaching. Betty had to hide their marriage, because she would have been fired. She said all these things critically, as though Betty and Rudy's current wealth was a sort of façade.

This particular Sunday, my mom and I had just returned from church. My mom was wearing her decent green church dress and her good stockings—no runs. Around the house, the rest of the week, she always wore torn stockings, so full of runs that I could never imagine how she got them on. After Betty and Rudy called, she disappeared upstairs. When she came back down to await their arrival, she wore a stained old house dress and her tattered stockings. I was both mystified and embarrassed. She was choosing to look poor.

The pattern becomes clearer. When my maternal grandfather died six months after my dad, my mother, again, showed no real emotion. She seemed not to grieve. But when my grandmother commented that she missed her husband of sixty years very much, my mother snapped, "What about me? I've lost both my husband and my father!" My grandmother looked startled. Yes, she conceded, it was true, you had two big losses. My mother seemed placated. Her pain always had to be the worst, and she needed to have it acknowledged.

Perversely, illness could be a good thing to my mother. She had been diagnosed with multiple sclerosis in the late 1960s. It was hard to diagnose—there were no definitive tests, just symptoms for the doctors to observe and evaluate. She had had double vision one brief time in her thirties. Then, in her late fifties, she began to feel unsteady on her feet, and her hands and feet often went numb. It was unclear, actually, how serious the symptoms were, because, to put it frankly, they seemed to suit her. It was convenient to have a disease she could blame, a disease that kept her indoors, a disease that sounded serious and crippling. She never pursued any therapies. I urged her to ask the doctor whether she really needed to quit driving, but she never did. The doctor suggested some medications, which she never pursued. Aunt Betty, a fan of diet guru Adele Davis, advocated vitamins and diet changes, but my mother ignored her. She gave up driving.

Her MS symptoms never drastically worsened, but when she fell and broke her hip in 1988, she ended up in a nursing home because she couldn't walk. She complained bitterly about the nursing home and always claimed she wanted to go home, but she never worked to make it happen. She did no physical therapy and spent all her time in bed or in a wheelchair. I felt frustrated, angry, and helpless when I visited her. She was miserable, but she refused to do anything to make herself feel better.

That nursing home had a big rotunda, available to rent for parties. My niece, Stephanie, decided to be married there. My mother opposed this wedding, just as she had objected to her daughters' weddings. She told me she was going to skip it and stay in her room and cry. She came after all and didn't cry, but she told several guests that the nursing home was her jail. Those people then dutifully reported this sad situation to my sister Marge, the mother of the bride. Marge's happiness for Stephanie was mixed with the familiar exasperation and frustration we so often felt about my mother.

Around that time, I told Marge, with some bitterness, that Mom now finally had the exact life she wanted. There was nothing she had to do, nowhere to go, and yet she could say constantly that she wanted to be somewhere else, and people would feel sorry for her. I think it pleased her when people thought she was poor, sick, and unlucky. Janice Cauwels, in *Imbroglio: Rising to the Challenges of Borderline Personality Disorder*, observes, "Borderlines appear to exaggerate their misery; they mope . . . The borderline feels misunderstood and unappreciated."

My mother seemed unable to differentiate between compassion and pity. The literature describes patients who envy suffering people, because they get all the love and attention that BPD sufferers crave. One writer describes a patient who fantasizes happily that a huge hospital has been built just for her.

I remember understanding, as a young child, that the terms *self-pity* and *feeling sorry for yourself* had negative connotations and at the same time noting how closely those terms fit my mom. When I was a kid, I once told her she complained a lot. Offended, she responded curtly, "I don't mean to complain," with a pained expression on her face. I knew not to say it again, but I continued to notice, and to feel bad about noticing.

I was always reminding myself of my mom's real misfortunes and all the things that made her feel bad. For example, because of our fixed income after the onset of my dad's illness, my mother lamented her inability get her hair done weekly like other women. My dad would answer calmly that she could get her hair done if she liked. She complained for many years about the worn state of our carpet, until my dad insisted she order a new one. He also purchased a color TV. It turned out that frequently we *could* afford things. I was confused—we bought things we needed or wanted, yet my mother always bemoaned our poverty.

When I was in high school, my mother was offered a job as the secretary to the president of a local college in Canton. Great, I thought. She'll be out and about and dressing up and meeting other people and bringing in some cash. My dad was pretty self-reliant, and I was in school all day. I imagined, for a minute, some big, positive changes in our household. Then she turned down the job. As my father explained in a letter to Betsey, "When she found out it was to be secretary to the prez., she chickened out because that would require perfection personified and overtime, which she did not feel she could fulfill with me and Kathy on her hands."

My mom had a bachelor's degree from Western Reserve University. After Reserve, she moved to New York and earned a Masters degree in French history from Columbia University. My sisters and I romanticized this achievement. How glamorous to go to New York by yourself. How admirable to go away to graduate school—as a woman in the 1930's, no less. When she came back, she lived at home until her marriage in 1941, at the age of twenty-nine. When my mother was horrorstruck at her daughters moving away after college, she was thinking of these years she spent at home, paying rent to her parents. For our part, we had always been inspired by Mom's fearlessly going off to New York for graduate school.

After graduate school, she taught at Collinwood High School in Cleveland for a semester, not an especially good experience. She always said disdainfully, "High school kids look at you like they're daring you to teach them something." Because it was the Depression, we were made to understand that the only other available jobs were secretarial jobs in offices, and so she taught stenography at a night school. She was an excellent typist and stenographer.

She had some highly marketable skills. I don't know how I would have felt to have a working mother, but at the time, I wished she would get a job. I think my father encouraged her to do so. Her refusal was, to me, a depressing affirmation of her continual and increasing tendency to let the world act on her, always negatively, and to avoid taking action to improve her situation, at the same time blaming life, or other people, for her sad state. "Borderlines work hard to be helpless," writes Janice M. Cauwels.

The later diagnosis of multiple sclerosis gave her even more reason to stay home. I was surprised to discover an entire passage in Robert G. Harper's *Personality-Guided Therapy in Behavioral Medicine* connecting borderline personality disorder and multiple sclerosis. Writing for professionals (that is, with a lot of jargon), Dr. Harper suggests what I had always suspected: that my mother might have been exploiting her diagnosis. "The most general effect of a prolonged episode of multiple sclerosis," he writes, "would be to create and justify greater dependency on the part of the patient and inhibit any expression of resentment on the part of the caretaker." He tactfully notes that "the vague and shifting nature of multiple sclerosis symptoms" makes it hard to distinguish "the subjective from true central nervous system pathology." So, when my mother complained that she had difficulty writing, I addressed her Christmas cards. When she resisted wrapping gifts and driving, I never knew if she really couldn't do these things or was just *choosing* not to do them. It drove me crazy. I wanted her to do more, but I couldn't blame her for being sick.

Once again, BPD helped clarify this issue for me, with the term "learned helplessness." A patient who has learned helplessness, according to Dr. Marsha Linehan, has given up altogether and "does not even try to get help from the environment."

Here's an example. One winter evening before Christmas, I sat on the living room floor wrapping dozens of gifts--for my sisters, brothers-in-law, and their kids. I had purchased them, and now I was wrapping them, and I felt resentful. I could see my mother sitting alone at her spot in the kitchen, fifteen feet away, listening to the radio, drinking coffee, and looking off into space.

What could I do to get her to help? Beyond my resentment, I was disturbed by the weirdness of the situation. Shouldn't a mother and daughter *enjoy* wrapping Christmas presents together? Shouldn't this be fun? What could I do to make her notice, to make her offer to help? I wanted her to be normal.

I selected several small, easy-to-wrap gifts and found an extra roll of tape and a pair of scissors. I cut off a swath of wrapping paper and took the whole collection into the kitchen and set them on the table. I was polite. "There's a lot to wrap," I said. "Could you help with a few things?"

My mother sighed doubtfully, but responded, "I suppose so." I returned to the living room and wrapped gifts by myself. She sat in the kitchen and wrapped everything I'd given her—awkwardly but well enough. Wrapping gifts in separate rooms was still weird and dysfunctional, but I had accomplished one goal: I had temporarily tamped down my resentment. Were her hands numb from the MS? Did they hurt? I didn't ask, and if I had I might not have believed her answer.

Either way, her inactivity—not driving and not shopping and not wrapping—seemed to suit her. At some point, she decided life was unfair and she was going to be unhappy. So, when it worked out that way, she seemed curiously satisfied.

Every year as Independence Day approached, you could count on my mother saying, "It's too bad. The Fourth of July means the summer's almost over." She hated the winter. She dreaded it, even though in her later years she virtually never went outside. She began dreading its return when it was barely over, with the very first signs of spring. Summer and sunny days were good, but she'd always point out that winter was on the horizon. Every summer, probably from the time I was in high school, I would dread the approach of the holiday because I knew the remark was coming.

She had a repertoire of depressing remarks. She often said, "Whenever someone says that things could be worse, they're really saying that things could be better." In other words, these other people were giving themselves false cheer. They were refusing to see how bad things really were. As adults, my sisters and I knew not to greet her by asking, "How are you?" The response would be a sigh, at best an "Okay," more often "Oh, you know," or "Not so good." We avoided many questions in order to shield ourselves from her despair.

When I graduated from college and started teaching, the standard July 4th remark truly rankled. Some teaching years were very hard; I hated going to work every day and *began* the school year virtually burned out. In those years, to hear my mother say that summer was almost over caused me physical pain. I remember taking care not to mention the Fourth to her in May or June so that I wouldn't have to hear it.

When I have repeated her sentiment to friends, they say, "That's silly. The Fourth is just the beginning of the summer." I know, I reply. For me, though, my mother's truth is partly my truth: the Fourth marks the beginning of the end of the summer.

Now, my son repeats it as a joke, but I still don't find it funny.

Occasionally I challenged my mother to think of something positive to say. Is there *anything* good about your life? I would ask. She would smile sadly or laugh humorlessly. If I could ask such a thing, then clearly I didn't understand how bad her life was. I was hurting her just by asking the question.

I struggle now to comprehend fully that my mother was suffering, not merely complaining. In *Borderline Personality Demystified*, Robert O. Friedel describes a 1994 study in which patients diagnosed with BPD were asked to describe themselves. Friedel's summary describes my mother:

> *They did not see themselves as having an illness, but as leading a life in which they constantly struggled against feelings of despair. This was a central theme of how they perceived their fate in the world . . . For the most part, they did not know the origins of these feelings . . . The sense of emotional pain and despair they reported was overwhelming. They all expressed the wish not to be alive.*

My mother feared snowstorms and watched TV weather reports assiduously to look out for them, even though she didn't have to go out. Rain made her sad. If you commented on a lovely day in April, my mother would invariably reply, "Yes, but it's not going to last."

From the time I was very small, lying in my bed, I heard her in the next room crying herself to sleep.

The "Turn"

(I)ndividuals with borderline personalities are characteristically erratic in their display of emotions, which are impulsively expressed or poorly modulated in response to the events around them. This leaves others mystified, shocked or repelled at the unpredictable nature of these individuals.

Robert G. Harper, *Personality-Guided Therapy in Behavioral Medicine*

In 1989, Marge's son Chad was killed in an automobile accident. He had played in an evening softball game and gone out with some friends afterwards. On the way home on a country road, the car in which he was riding swerved off the pavement. The young men in the car were thrown out, and the car rolled over and struck Chad's head. Later tests showed that Chad had not been drinking. The other two in the car, including the driver, had been drinking but were not hurt. Chad was 19.

When Marge called to tell me what had happened, I hurried to Canton and accompanied her and Betsey to the nursing home to tell my mother. This was not so much to support my mom as to support Marge. We all understood that telling my mother would be difficult, not because she would react emotionally but because she probably wouldn't. We realized intuitively she wouldn't know how to comfort Marge and might even say something undermining. Only a few months before, Marge had been diagnosed with breast cancer and had chosen not to tell our mother. Not because she didn't want to upset her, but because she knew not to expect any encouragement.

Now, Marge needed us with her. Somehow we all knew this without anyone saying it.

The forewarned staff had reserved a private meeting room for us. When Marge told my mother what had happened, she responded with, "Oh, dear," and other appropriate words, but showed little emotion. Marge began to talk to me and Betsey while my mother sat by silently.

66

Marge described her gratitude for the previous morning. She and Chad had been up early and watched a little of the *Today* show together before they both went off to work. There had been something funny to talk about, and they had laughed together and had a simple, pleasant conversation at a time of day when they usually didn't cross paths. Marge said, "It was lucky that was our last time together, because I could just as easily have been yelling at him to clean his room."

Suddenly my mom was roused from her silence. "Well," she said emphatically, "at least I never did anything like that to you girls."

My sisters and I looked at each other, appalled, and then laughed darkly. First, we were shocked that my mother would say something so unsympathetic, so "off," so out of tune. But her remark was also patently untrue. Of course, she yelled at us, often precisely about cleaning our rooms. She raged at us. We all remember her desperate shrieking, "Kids!" She would shout it as though she was sorry we'd ever been born.

Somehow, in my mother's mind, that moment, as Marge talked about losing her son, was precisely the time to insist that she had been a better mother, that she had never lost control, that she had never said the wrong thing to her children. Christine Anne Lawson writes, "One of the most devastating experiences for children of borderlines is 'The Turn.' The Turn is a sudden attack, the abrupt withdrawal of love and affection, and razor-sharp words that can pierce the heart as painfully as an arrow."

My mom was the past master of The Turn, wherein a conversation lurches off the sunny footpath into the dark undergrowth nearby. Out of nowhere, she'd remind you that you never helped out around the house or that your room was always a mess. She never *made* us do chores. It was always that we *chose* not to do them, thereby disappointing her. She told us that she and my dad tried to make lots of noise as they washed the dishes, hoping we would hear and offer to help. But no, she said, we were too lazy. Decades later, she could call up our failures.

She complained bitterly, not only about our dog Abbie, but also about our long-lived cat Gray Girl. The cat spent the last few months of her eighteen years sleeping on a pile of grocery bags in my mother's kitchen. One day, she got up and walked slowly to the back door to be let out. My mom opened the door for her, and she never came back. When she was younger, Gray Girl used to curl up next to my mom while she watched TV. Like many cats, she seemed perversely drawn to people who didn't like her. My mom would frown and shake her head but allow the cat to stay. Once, I remarked about my mother hating cats, and she responded impatiently, "What do you mean? I've always had a cat. I don't hate cats!" Bewildering, again. Was it just Gray Girl she hated? Once again, I felt blindsided by her furious response.

I've been realizing lately that I'm *always*, even now, steeled for The Turn. I don't necessarily expect people to express their dark thoughts like my mom did, but I imagine the dark thoughts they're hiding behind their friendly exteriors. Worrying about what others are thinking is a residual effect of growing up in my mother's house. I knew she was harboring dark thoughts about me and my behavior. For example, she had a proprietary attitude about everything she owned. I could borrow her things and use them. She might even give them to me. But at some point, she was sure to comment pointedly that they belonged to her, not me. She let me drive her car, but frequently noted that it was hers. She lent Marge money, but constantly reminded her of the debt. She allowed Betsey's family to live with her for a time, but made her kids feel like unwelcome guests.

Even our own belongings weren't really our own. When I shared my delight in cashing a paycheck, she'd comment that it wasn't really my money, even though I had earned it, because, after all, I could never pay her back for all the money she had spent on me. Exasperated, I once asked her, Does that mean that for the rest of my life I can never have my own money? All of it is really yours? She laughed uncomfortably, but answered quite seriously that yes, that was the crux of it. The next time I expressed pleasure in something I'd bought or money I'd earned, she might not repeat this distressing remark. But I'd know she was thinking it.

If I made an innocuous observation about the dog or cat, she might comment that she had never wanted them, but she was stuck with them. If I confessed a weakness or fault, she would say that she never had that problem. Once in high school I confided that I was forgetful and disorganized, which troubled me at school. She looked dumbfounded, said it wasn't true, and asserted that *she* had certainly never had that problem, as though that ended it. After I became a mother, if I complained good-naturedly about my babies crying or keeping me awake at night, she would say her babies were perfect and never did that. When I recalled that, in the past, she was often unhappy or inaccessible as I was growing up, or remembered that she yelled at us, she'd deny it.

To put it mildly, my mother was undermining. I once told her how meaningful it would be to hear her say she was proud of us. "Of course, I'm proud of you," she said indignantly. "Why should I have to say it?" As the perfect mother, unable to admit a mistake, she insisted she was proud of me, because good mothers are proud of their children. At the same time, I was given to understand that by asking the question I had let her down once again.

Again

[B]orderline patients may be so rigid, so numbed, so distant, so closed off . . . that they spend large portions of their lives in a state akin to shock.

Roger A. Lewin and Clarence Schulz, *Fusing and Losing: Borderline Transitional Object and Self Relations*

Five years after Chad's death, my family suffered a nightmarish déjà vu, when my niece Karen, Betsey's oldest child, was killed in an automobile accident. She and her friend, both students at Xavier University in Cincinnati, went out to the mall on a day so cold that classes had been canceled. When they pulled out of the mall onto the highway, their car skidded across several lanes into the path of an SUV. Karen, the passenger, was killed instantly.

So much seemed the same. Choosing clothes and picking out a casket for a young person. Making calls to relatives and friends. The haunted faces of young people walking into a funeral home. My sisters holding it together.

So also the trip to the nursing home. The three of us went together again. This time we met my mother in her room. When Betsey told her what had happened, my mother said, "No. Not Karen."

She kept repeating, "I can't believe it. I just don't believe it's true." This didn't sound like the normal shock anyone would feel. For my mother, the words seemed literally true. She just couldn't take in such news.

Rene J. Muller, an emergency room psychiatrist, writes this about borderline patients: "It is impossible to mourn successfully and get over the loss of anyone, or anything, until the true meaning of what has been lost is fully acknowledged." My mother seemed unable to acknowledge true loss.

A couple of weeks after Karen's death, my mom came down with a serious flu, as she had after the death of my father. It was gratifying. It showed that, somewhere, she was reacting. Somewhere, she was hurting, and if her mind and spirit couldn't express it, her body would.

Interlude

You're probably a better judge of character than you think, if you allow yourself to listen to your gut reaction.

Kimberlee Roth, *Surviving a Borderline Parent*

My learning about borderline personality disorder proceeded, deepening over time, especially as I began writing. I was beginning not just to know the symptoms but to *feel* them. One evening in 2007 John and I saw a film directed by Noah Baumbach, *Margot at the Wedding*. Baumbach's previous film, *The Squid and the Whale,* concerned a family in which the divorcing parents are so self-absorbed that they do pretty much everything wrong with respect to their children. Supposedly, the script was at least partly autobiographical, and the father in the film is pretty much a narcissist. In Baumbach's subsequent film, Nicole Kidman plays Margot, a tactless, self-absorbed writer who says every negative thing that comes into her mind, especially to her sister (Jennifer Jason Leigh), who's about to marry a sad-sack loser (Jack Black).

Margot is very close to her twelve-year-old son. At first this closeness is touching, but then it becomes unsettling. She confides in him inappropriately, complaining about family members and telling him that his aunt is pregnant, even though she has been sworn to secrecy. She's generally erratic, sometimes funny and affectionate, sometimes hypercritical. In one scene, she turns to her son and unexpectedly castigates him for not being helpful enough. All the other cousins are so helpful, why not him? He is taken aback. He tries to defend himself and at the same time seems to believe what his mother says, because after all she's his mother. "It's The Turn," I thought to myself. In that moment, I identified perfectly with the child. I whispered, "Borderline," to my husband beside me.

A few scenes later, Jennifer Jason Leigh's character screams out her frustration at her sister's constant criticism. She yells at Margot, "And everyone says you have borderline personality disorder!" I elbowed John.

Spreading the Pain Around

I just want you to hurt like I do.
Randy Newman, "Honest I Do"

A typical exchange would go like this. We're sitting in the kitchen, tensely silent. My mother has just told me that I'm breaking her heart by dating the divorced John M. She can't sleep. She can't understand what's happened to me. What happened to her perfect daughter? Why do I not care about her? She shakes her head, and cries, and looks enraged at every response I offer. She's glad, she says at last, that my father isn't there to see my behavior. He was a puritan, she tells me. He was conservative about morals and marriage and divorce. He would be ashamed, she says, to know I was dating a divorced man.

My dad had died only two years before. I still feel sad and guilty about my silence during his illness and write in my journal and pray and cry frequently about failing him. I miss him all the time and find my mother all the more difficult to deal with, without him there as a buffer. Hearing that my dad would be ashamed of me is the harshest thing my mother could say to me.

I try, as always, to consider the truth of what she's saying. She's my mother, and so, a part of me believes her. My dad would have disapproved, I assume, and would have worried about me. I think he also would have expressed his concerns more reasonably than my mom. He would not have cried and screamed; he would not have called me names. When I consider how compassionately and sympathetically he championed Marge, I realize that he would have showed me the same understanding.

So, I try again with my mother. I explain how painful this particular argument is. I tell her, "I hear what you're saying, and there's no way I'm going to forget it. But you should understand how much it hurts me for you to say that Dad would be ashamed of me. I've heard you and will think about what you've said. Just never say that particular thing again."

A fleeting and enigmatic expression crosses my mother's face. I can't parse her discomfiting expression. She doesn't look indignant or offended; still less, compassionate and understanding. To say she looks pleased would be going too far, but perhaps I see a split second of satisfaction.

In any event, my plea has no effect. She repeats the remark about my dad often. Though I know her well, this always surprises me. Why does she lash out? Why does she deliberately choose to say the most wounding thing she can?

Decades later, my friendship with Nancy provides some

insight. She sent me a bitter email, describing a startling recollection. Twenty years before, long before I had a clue about her underlying issues, she had asked me a question. Someone interrupted us, and I never got around to answering. She still felt the pain, she told me, and she had never forgiven me.

The next day I called to tell her I didn't enjoy reading such a harsh message, and I wondered about that memory. She had never forgiven me *for neglecting to answer a question*? She had carried this with her all these years, without my knowing? I was sorry, I said, but beyond that, what was I supposed to do with this information?

"I don't know what you're supposed to do with it," she said reasonably, never having thought of it from my point of view. She knew the pain caused by the memory was disproportionate. She knew that she shouldn't still be angry. She was just trying to convey the pain she always felt.

"I don't want you to feel bad," she said. "I wasn't trying to hurt your feelings."

"Of course not," I responded. "I know you're not *trying* to hurt my feelings." I explained that now I realized she had been harboring this grudge all the time, feeling snubbed as though it had just happened yesterday.

She was sorry. She repeated that she hadn't meant to hurt me.

Then, suddenly, she switched gears. "You know," she said thoughtfully. "I *was* trying to hurt you."

Taken aback, but impressed by her honesty, I said, "Okay. Why is that?"

"I think it's because I don't believe anyone can understand how I'm hurting unless they're hurting, too."

"I'm hurting so much," she went on. "It was so hard for me to go out of my way to talk to you back then. And when you didn't answer, it was like a slap in the face. It still hurts me to think about it. But how could you ever understand that unless I hurt you, too?"

It was as though my mother had returned to explain herself to me.

My sisters and I have often commented that my mother believed she was powerless. She thought we didn't listen. She had no idea how deeply her words wounded us. She thought she had to lash out just to have any effect at all.

But now, as though channeling my mother, Nancy had explained why. My mother was in pain. She was always in pain and was hurting even more because I was threatening to abandon her. No one could know how much she hurt. But if she passed on a little pain, if she struck out, if she flailed around and made a few barbs stick, maybe someone would share a tiny bit of her pain and she wouldn't feel so alone.

Now I see BPD everywhere. My husband and friends mock me because, suddenly, I see it all around—in old relationships, in movies, in books. I can't read Ann Patchett's *Truth and Beauty* now without seeing my mother in Patchett's demanding and frustrating friend Lucy Grealy. When I read Augusten Burroughs' wrenching memoirs *Running with Scissors* and *A Wolf at the Table*, I think, of course, his abusive father had borderline personality disorder.

I discover parents with BPD in the novels I read. Liz, a character in Margaret Drabble's *The Radiant Way*, calling her depressed mother a "domestic ghost," eventually comes to respect "how bleakly and boldly [her mother] has stared over the years into the heart of nothingness."

In Alice Sebold's *The Almost Moon*, a frustrated adult daughter smothers her recalcitrant, critical mother in a moment of rage. "It was my mother's disappointments that were enumerated in our household," Sebold writes, "and that I saw before me every day as if they were posted on our fridge—a static list that my presence could not assuage." I recognize the mother, and I recognize the rage.

Feeling Stuck

It is certainly the anecdote that counts. Not the moral, the point, or the interpretation. If just the particulars can be kept clear, then there will be a kind of thing made, something to see . . . The interpretations may then be as numerous as readers.

James Herndon, *The Way It Spozed to Be*

At some points in this writing, I stall for awhile. My fund of memories seems to run dry. No more stories come to mind--just snippets of memories, words spoken, patterns. I worry that I've run out of evidence, because I want to prove my mother's diagnosis. I have to justify it on the page, and I have little psychologists on my shoulders, whispering, "Not really borderline. You're making it up."

To fill the empty spaces, I check out as many library books on BPD as I can find. Sometimes, I have as many as a dozen at once. They litter the coffee table and the floor and my desk. They're all helpful, except maybe for one with a feminist slant. It claims that women are over-diagnosed with BPD as an aspect of our general oppression. That may be true, but I don't want to hear it. I want my mother to have had BPD because it's helping me so much to see her in this light. Believing she was ill, that she couldn't help the things she did, is like a balm; it literally soothes the rough, wounded places inside me. I crave validation, giving me some empathy for Nancy's need, and also my mother's.

All of the books, however, lose me at times. My mother didn't rush out to bars and pick up men. She wasn't reckless. Maybe she drank too much for a period of her life. The way she spent money was a little weird. But there was no "acting out," in current psychological terms.

Still, the most frequently discussed characteristics—the splitting and fear of abandonment and emptiness and dysphoria—are so telling. These are words that explain her to me. They contain so much about her that I never spoke aloud to anyone. They explain things that weighed on me so heavily. As the spiritual writer

Kathleen Norris writes in *Acedia & Me,* "As any reader of fairy tales can tell you, not knowing the true name of your enemy, be it a troll, a demon or an 'issue,' puts you at a great disadvantage, and learning the name can help to set you free."

At last, when I'm stuck, I realize I'm reading the books to find her. I skim the pages, not giving any individual book enough time, looking for my mother. And then I realize she's not in the books. All I can find of her is inside me—what I see in myself and what I find in my memories. My sisters can help.

I keep losing track of my first intent. This line from James Herndon inspires me and keeps me on track: "It is certainly the anecdote that counts." In writing about his years of teaching, Herndon, a career middle-school teacher, tells hilarious, outrageous, and sometimes painful stories. He doesn't expound theories, he doesn't argue cases. He lets his unique, sometimes wild students and the intransigent bureaucracy he works for present his case. You make of it what you will.

I can write about myself, and I can write about her. I feel like taking memories out like objects and setting them on the table in front of me. There I can look at them; I can study them from different angles. I can show them to other people and ask, "What do you think about that? Was that crazy, or is it me? Is that normal?"

In the years up to now, I've been trying to answer these questions inside my head, trying to see these objects in my brain, not holding them up to the light where they can be seen. I witnessed my mother doing this very thing: living in isolation, talking only to strike out or to make idle chit-chat or to accuse. I saw it in Nancy, before her therapy and her struggle to get better, sometimes striving to solve her problems inside her own head, turning big problems around in that small space, instead of bringing them out to be looked at straight, with reason and calmness. She believed she had to solve her problems all by herself. Sometimes she believed, like my mother, that everyone should understand what she was thinking without her having to tell them.

Now I'm trying to take out the memories, dust them off, and examine them. I'll study each one like the shapes on the SAT. How would it look from this angle? What does it look like now, after ten, twenty, thirty years? Can I tell what it means?

While I'm writing, then getting stuck, then writing some more, then feeling guilty about exposing my mom and my family, getting stuck again, I see Francois Truffaut's *The Four Hundred Blows*, which I haven't seen for thirty years. This painful autobiographical first film dramatizes his difficult childhood and deeply flawed parents. I drive home in tears. I'm not Truffaut. But if, like him, I try to be fair and I try to be loving, I can tell my own story.

Damned If You Do . . .

No, you can't win. I will win. I'll get you coming and I'll get you going and there will be no way that you can win. I must always win.

A.J. Mahari, BPD patient

When I was in college, I read an excerpt from Philip Roth's *The Breast* in my mom's *Atlantic Monthly*. I thought she would be gratified that I was reading her magazines. Feeling grown up, I foolishly mentioned to her how much I was enjoying *The Breast*, even though, I acknowledged, the language and subject matter were a little shocking.

My mother snapped, "So that's why you're reading it? You *like* the bad language?"

There were no good choices. I felt this throughout my childhood, long before I could have verbalized it. If we did no housework, if we didn't help out, we were lazy and unappreciative. If we tried to clean up, we were implicitly criticizing my mother, or moving her things, or throwing something away she might have needed. I can't remember a finished chore being acknowledged or appreciated. Tasks undone were catalogued, but a cleaned room or a mowed lawn went unremarked.

It was impossible to do the right thing, because whatever you chose turned out to be wrong.

"Borderlines put you in a position in which you feel a certain way," says Janice Cauwels, "and have been maneuvered into saying something . . . , and then they cream you for it." How often I felt creamed. When we were enmeshed in our fights about my college boyfriend, I once imagined I had found a logical solution to my mother's concerns. I reasoned that the real problem, according to the Catholic Church, is not with divorce, but with remarriage. I intuited fairly early on that John M. was not the man of my dreams. He was gentle and nice, but he rarely made me laugh. He was intelligent, but winced if I used a word he didn't know, so I was always censoring my vocabulary. I couldn't speak naturally for fear of inadvertently making him feel dumb. And who knows why else? I just knew deep down that this relationship would end. I knew we wouldn't marry.

I thought this news would comfort my mom. After long, harrowing arguments in which my mother would rail about divorce and fret about my reputation and my eternal soul, I would reassure her. But, Mom, I would say, I'm not going to marry him. She was appalled, rather than placated. "Why are you seeing him, then? Are you just stringing him along?" she would hiss. I was even more decadent than she had imagined: dating a guy, "enjoying" him in who knows what degenerate way, with no intention of marrying him.

I couldn't win. When I decided to seek an assistantship for graduate school, the application required a parent's signature. When I asked her to sign it, she responded, "You won't do what I want you to do. Why should I help you when you ask?" Her signature, she said, would represent just one more debt I owed her. Without another word, I sealed the envelope, sent off the form, and received the assistantship anyway. Two years later, I needed surgery. The hospital bill was $1,000, and I arranged to pay $100 a month, a strain on my meager budget, but doable. I preferred paying the bill myself to hearing about another obligation I could never fulfill.

In both cases, she eventually let me know that I had hurt her terribly by rejecting her help.

Once, years later, when I was visiting my mom in the nursing home, her friendly roommate, Rose, picked up her phone to call her daughter. My mother scoffed and shook her head at me. "She talks to her daughters three or four times a day," she said disapprovingly, as though Rose was wasting her time.

Then she added pointedly, "Of course, my daughters *never* call me." So, first, Rose's frequent talks with her daughters were silly. A second later, they became an opportunity to chastise me and my sisters for rarely calling her.

At the same time, of course, we had both observed Rose calling her daughter, not vice versa. I pointed out that Rose had actually dialed up her daughter, something that my mother was always free to do but never did. I could count on the fingers of one hand, literally, the number of times my mother called me on the phone. In my whole life, my mother called me, perhaps, five times.

She just shook her head in response. These exchanges were always unsatisfying. My mother would just quit talking, as though giving up on my ever understanding.

I couldn't win. How often I felt I was saying or doing something right, only to get sucker-punched. When I left the house, I'd get a doleful look. "What?" I'd say. "You don't want me to go out?" My mother would shrug and say sadly, "No, go ahead," achieving (I assumed) her goal of making me feel guilty. When my sisters and I would ask when we should come home, she would respond, "At a reasonable hour." Suffice it to say, we rarely chose an hour she found reasonable.

Once again, the BPD literature rescues me, reassuring me that I wasn't crazy or imagining things. Therapists must constantly negotiate these lose-lose situations. Say, for example, the therapist is going on vacation. If he or she tells the borderline patient ahead of time, the patient has lots of time to become anxious. If the therapist waits until the last minute, the patient won't have enough time to prepare. If he or she tries not telling the patient at all, there is hell to pay when the therapist gets back.

Family and friends are in a similar quandary. If you call the person with BPD, you're trying to evade a face-to-face visit. If you write instead of call, you don't want to talk. If you call when she's not home, you purposely dodged her. If you avoid calling for fear of recriminations, well, she was waiting by the phone.

This, however, is a one-sided perspective. The perspective of the person with BPD is one of anxiety and chaos. The quote at the beginning of this chapter comes from a lengthy on-line rant composed by a person in recovery, A.J. Mahari, to demonstrate the conflicting, raging, anxious thoughts of the person with borderline. So, I am trying to comprehend the alternate reality of the sufferer, overwhelmed with confusing thoughts and powerful, irrational feelings. I am trying to comprehend that my mother was not deliberately manipulative, not purposely screwing with me and my sisters. She couldn't help the things she did. This is the concept I am working to get my mind around. "Lose-lose" is a result of the borderline condition, not the sufferer's deliberate choice.

When my mom still lived alone in her house, and I lived in Canton as a young married woman, I did her grocery shopping for her. Though I pretty much knew what she needed every week, I would usually omit at least one important thing. I'd mistakenly believe she still had enough frozen vegetables or eggs to last her for a few more days.

Because I'd inevitably forget some crucial item, I'd be forced to make another trip to the store. And I had to make that extra stop, because at one point my mom wasn't eating right, like a lot of elderly people, and had to be hospitalized. So my sisters and I became quite conscientious about making sure she had the right things to eat at home.

After a couple of these extra trips, I began calling her before I left for the store to ask what she needed. There'd be a long pause. Then she'd say, "Well, the usual things. I need a loaf of bread, and I'm almost out of eggs. Get me some hamburger and some of those minute steaks I like." She might list a few more things that I dutifully wrote down. I'd say I was leaving soon, so if she thought of anything else she should call me back.

I'd arrive at her house an hour or two later. As we unloaded the bags in her kitchen, my mother would look pained. "What?" I'd ask.

"You didn't get any bananas," she'd say.

"But you didn't tell me bananas."

"I thought of it after we hung up."

"So, why didn't you call me back?"

"I didn't want to bother you."

We had some version of that conversation frequently.

Shopping for my mom, in general, was fraught with the danger of recriminations, involving as it did the spending of her money. From the time I was in high school and for many years after, I decorated my mother's house for Christmas and did her holiday shopping as well. I would ask her for some guidelines about how much to spend. What did she want me to buy for my sisters and their husbands and the grandchildren?

"Oh, I don't know," my mother would say. "Just buy what you think they'd like."

I felt burdened by this responsibility, but I'll also admit to enjoying it. Shopping can be fun, and it was especially fun to shop double, buying my own gifts and my mom's, for my nieces and nephews. So, I enjoyed the buying. I also believed I was helping my mother.

When I brought home the bags of gifts, feeling pleased about my purchases, she usually had a lukewarm reaction. She would nod and look away, or smile awkwardly, as though playacting the required response. Any gift for my brothers-in-law elicited a frown. Then I would ask impatiently, "Do you *want* to get them anything at all?" I never got a straight answer.

Generally, I never knew if I had spent too much, bought the wrong things, made her feel bad for some other reason, or actually done a good job.

Finally, one year, when I was enthusiastically displaying my purchases, my mother suddenly looked angry. She stopped me short with this comment: "You sure enjoy spending my money, don't you?"

Another example of The Turn. It's the moment when one

thinks everything's fine and she cuts you to the quick.

All this time, I should have been somewhere else, I suppose. I stayed stuck at home for too long, uncertain what to do with my life. Stagnant, shy, worried about hurting her, paralyzed.

I honestly felt that she appreciated having me at home after my dad's death. I shopped, I cleaned, I mowed the lawn, I watched TV with her. But often when I went out, she would greet my return with, "So, you just left me with all the phone messages. I guess I'm your secretary."

Or she would say, "I hope you enjoyed driving my car."

I should have gotten out sooner. I went to graduate school largely to get away from her to pursue a goal she couldn't possible criticize me for, having left home for graduate school herself.

When I was ten or eleven, I ran across some booklets about menstruation that my older sisters had gotten at school. I grabbed and read them eagerly, but also with a nagging sense that I was doing something wrong. I hid them under my mattress for safe-keeping.

Mothers always find things kids hide under their mattress, don't they? And my mother was normal in that she made our beds.

She said to me sadly, "I found those books you were reading and hid in your room." Clearly I had disappointed her, but I wasn't sure why. Because I had read them? Because I had hidden them? Because I hadn't come to her with questions?

She continued, "If you want to know more, there's a book on the kitchen counter in an envelope. You can get it out and read it when you want to. Tell me if you have any questions."

So, in my little pre-adolescent heart, I saw this as a step forward. My mom wanted to share some of this verboten information with me, even if she couldn't do it face to face. Soon after, when she was out of the kitchen, I found the book on the shelf. It was a volume that the Catholic diocese distributed to parents to help them explain sex to children. It was—I'm not kidding—in a plain brown envelope.

I wish now that I had stashed that book away and kept it forever. I'd love to have it now to quote from. I remember reading something about men offering themselves up on the altar of their wives' bodies, and I don't think I could have made that up. But it also contained useful, clear information—all the basics about puberty for both boys and girls. The format was largely idealized dialogue between attentive, articulate parents and curious kids. Even then, I sensed the irony of *reading* a warm and candid conversation between parent and child instead of actually *having* one. I also felt guilty for learning so much about boys' bodies, including penis size and wet dreams. I wasn't sure that a girl my age was supposed to know all that, but there it was in the book, and I was curious. I felt guilty about my curiosity, but I also remembered that my mom had directed me to the book. She had almost encouraged me to ask her questions about it!

A day or two went by, and then my mother approached me at bedtime. "Well," she said regretfully, "you certainly didn't waste any time looking for that book, did you? I see it's gone from the shelf already." Her reproachful expression was very sad and very familiar.

Thinking in Black and White

Dichotomous thinking is the tendency to evaluate experiences in terms of mutually exclusive categories (e.g., good or bad, success or failure, trustworthy or deceitful) rather than seeing experiences as falling along continua. . . . There are no intermediate categories.

Aaron T. Beck and Arthur Freeman, *Cognitive Therapy of Personality Disorders*

My dad began criticizing Lyndon Johnson's escalation of the

Vietnam War early on, in 1965 or so. My mom disagreed, and they would argue about the war. My dad complained that he had voted for Johnson as the peace candidate and against the trigger-happy Goldwater. How disheartening that the candidate who promised not to send our boys to fight in Asia was now shipping them off by the boatload. My mother would claim that we had to honor our commitments to Vietnam. My dad would insist, "But, Eleanore, they don't even want us there!"

My mother, a dyed-in-the-wool Democrat, proudly voted for the first time in 1932, when Franklin Roosevelt first ran for president. She spoke of FDR reverently, almost worshipfully, and she loved and admired Eleanor, too. It's true that lots of people of my mom's generation revered the Roosevelts. I admire them myself. But my mom would brook no criticism; FDR was perfect.

Every subsequent Democrat received not only her vote, but her devotion as well. Truman, Stevenson, Kennedy, Johnson, Carter—she admired them all. Notable, in retrospect, is her inability to see any shades of gray.

I suspect now that my mother, in her desperate defensiveness, was unable to acknowledge *anything* mistaken or bad in a Democratic administration. There could be no middle ground— to commit any wrongdoing or to admit any mistake was to be bad. Perfect or evil, those were the choices. As years went on, and the consensus seemed to grow that Vietnam had been a mistake, my mom's last resort was to put it all on the Republican Eisenhower. After all, he was the one, she would say, who'd made the commitments and sent the first advisors.

I noted the same intransigence when the sexual peccadilloes of some of these Democrats made the news. Before my mother died, Kennedy's numerous affairs and Roosevelt's relationship with Lucy Mercer, his wife's secretary, had become common knowledge. If the topic came up, my mother would scoff and change the subject, or insist they were just rumors. Surely it's hard for any true-blue loyalist to concede fault in her heroes, but I found it odd that an educated woman like my mom couldn't concede that members of her party had faults.

She was capable of more complex thinking with respect

to the Catholic Church. Having learned in college about the Church's historical scandals, she would impatiently try to convince my grandmother that all of the popes weren't perfect. I suspect, however, that my mom's rational approach to Church history would have stopped short of more recent times. If I had pushed her about the Church's dilatory response to Nazism, or alluded to Christian anti-Semitism, or pointed out any corruption or flaw in a twentieth-century pope, I imagine she would have pushed back. It was okay to find flaws in the distant past, but I think she would have had trouble with the present day.

Black-and-white thinking is a hallmark of BPD. It forces people to make extreme interpretations of events and drastic re-evaluations of their loved ones' character. A loving, trustworthy, person becomes completely unreliable the first time he or she disappoints. As Dr. Beck writes, "The idea that a person might be trustworthy *most of the time* would be incompatible with dichotomous thinking." In much of the literature, this symptom is called splitting.

I fell victim to my mom's splitting, of course, as I changed from a perfect daughter to a bitter disappointment. I had seen it happen before me, when my sisters let my mom down by flunking out of college, getting pregnant, and moving away. My mom was clearly thinking dichotomously when she described her marriage: before my dad's illness, it had been a fairy tale. After his illness, but before he died, she became a widow, and her life a nightmare.

Despite her intelligence, my mother blamed my father for her unhappiness. Dichotomous thinking creates a storm of conflict in the mind. Everything has to have a cause, every problem is someone's fault. Most often, people suffering with BPD ultimately blame themselves for everything wrong with their lives. Though they may seem to lash out at others, though they are prone to anger, they have a sneaking suspicion that they really have only themselves to blame. Dr. Beck puts it this way:

(T)he borderlines' dichotomous categorization of themselves (as well as others) as either flawless or completely unacceptable leads to the conclusion that if they have any shortcomings, they are irrevocably "not OK." *The conviction that they are inherently unac-ceptable leadsquickly to the conclusion that they must hide this fact from others in order to be accepted.*

Tragically, people with BPD tend to avoid authentic intimacy (though not necessarily sexual intimacy) because their horrific (to them) flaws might be discovered. When they consequently feel lonely and abandoned, their black-and-white thinking leads them to believe that they'll *never* get what they want and that *all* of life is meaningless and miserable. If they try to confront their own defects, they can't help "discovering" that they're totally de-fective.

My mother does not fit this description in one important re-spect: she does not demonstrate the typical borderline self-hatred. My sisters and I agree that my mother exhibited little self-doubt. It seems unlikely to us that she felt "inherently unacceptable." Al-though we know little of her inner life and it's possible she was tormented by low self-esteem, we have no evidence. My mother seems to have gone to the other extreme. Sometimes, according to experts, the person with BPD operates under the assumption that he or she is perfect, for the same reason that others regard themselves as fatally flawed: they are unable to tolerate ambiguity.

In her mind, my mother was the perfect parent. She never yelled at her kids. She was always right. She was well-intentioned. She fulfilled her duties as a daughter, a wife, and a mother. She desperately clung to the unambiguous view that she was flawless.

Hence, dichotomous thinking can make a person difficult to live with. I can remember only one time that my mother apolo-gized to me, and I cherish the memory. It happened early in our conflict over the boyfriend, the devil endangering her daughter's soul. We had had a bitter argument. When I returned to school, I received a brief note from my mom, one of only a few I ever received from her. It said,

Hope you made it to Kent this morning without incident. I've been thinking, as I didn't before, I thought too little and talked too much. Now, I feel I must go back to my first reaction, which I believe

*is fairer to you and therefore much more comfortable for me. I hope
I have not taken too much time to reach that decision. Blame it on
a crazy, mixed up mother, who should have known you better.*

Even so, the conflict, as I have said, raged on for years, and
my mother's bitterness only increased. It never went away. It so-
lidified in her mind into an unbearable, indelible memory of loss,
shame, and betrayal. Like my sisters, I was variously a disappointment, a loser, and even a slut. But when my mother wrote and
mailed that apology, she was behaving like a reasonable and loving person. I'm so glad I still have that note.

Passivity and Emptiness

*Deepening of love requires that love be returned. If you feel empty
inside, you are likely to feel that you have little to give or that any effort to
give will leave you completely drained.*

Richard A. Moskovitz, *Lost in the Mirror:
An Inside Look at Borderline Personality Disorder*

On rare occasions, Marge left her kids with my mom for a
few hours. Stephanie and Chad would play outside or upstairs. I
stopped by on some of those afternoons. My mother would be sitting in her usual kitchen chair. "Where are the kids?" I would ask.

"Oh, I haven't seen them," she would say. "I think they're outside somewhere."

My niece and nephew were old enough that I didn't really
worry about their safety, although I thought my mother should
at least know where they were. What struck me was that she paid
them almost no attention. It never occurred to her to play with
them, read to them, do a craft, or bake something special for
them. They were on their own.

Some of my friends are new grandparents. My own kids, now
grown, could marry and have kids at any time. I have a glimmer

of how delightful grandkids can be. I love babies. I would enjoy helping my kids with their own children. I'd love to buy things for my grandchildren and take them places and cook with them and play with them. I witness the joy my sisters take in their grandchildren and see a similar delight in my friends who've become grandparents.

My mother derived a little pleasure from her grandchildren. I found a comment in my journals that I'm glad I recorded, because otherwise I would never have believed my mother had said it. I was describing a trip to the nursing home with my daughter, Margaret, who was about two. She was toddling around, smiling at the other residents, charming them. My mother seemed pleased and said, "How did you get to have such a cute little girl? She's even cuter than you were, and I never thought I'd say that." My mother could be pleasant about little kids and enjoyed reminiscing about us when we were very small.

When I was pregnant, she seemed pleased in a distant sort of way. Same thing when I brought my babies to see her. She'd smile, but she'd never reach for them or ask to hold them. If I suggested it, she'd hold them—uncomfortably. She liked them all right, but she behaved as though they had no relationship to her, as if they were somebody else's grandchildren. She seemed abstracted. She seemed to be playacting.

She was the same with my sisters' kids: smiling, saying some of the right things, but never engaged. My sisters and I vividly remember an oft-repeated remark regarding grandparenthood. We heard her say a thousand times when we were growing up that grandparents should not be relied on as babysitters. Parents shouldn't dump their kids on the grandparents. So, in general, my mother didn't babysit.

People with BPD, the experts say, suffer chronic feelings of emptiness. People with the disorder talk of having a hole inside, a lack of life, and use relationships to fill up that hole. My mother didn't seem to lack an identity or to be unsure of herself exactly, but there was something empty about her.

I have no access to my mother's inner life. I can't know

what she was feeling, but know only what I observed. *Emptiness* sounds right to me. In 1971, a few months after my father died, I wrote about my frustration with my mom, the draining effect I felt. At the time, I didn't understand what it meant. I didn't understand I was describing emptiness.

My problem with Mom has nothing to do with loving her or even agreeing with her. It's just that she's so inhuman, vegetable. She doesn't notice how you look or how or why you're saying something or how you're different or if what you're saying is not good or especially good. It's like living with a half-human. She's sort of both entirely objective and entirely subjective. Entirely objective in that she's completely opinion-less and emotion-less and preference-less, except in very predictable ways—you know what TV shows she prefers, that she doesn't ever want to drive, or let you go much of any-place. She operates by formula.

And in that she has no picture of herself—she can't see how she looks or sounds or appeared in a certain situation. I was thinking how she probably doesn't think of memories of her and Dad with a picture in her mind of how they both looked—she's not agonizing over memories like getting mad at him or digging at him for not being able to work in the garden, etc., etc., because she's like an animal—no self-awareness.

Entirely subjective in that in a certain way she thinks only of herself. If her formula—not wanting to call someplace, a gas station or something—runs into conflict with something else--my not wanting to—she can't resolve it. She can only force herself, if I'm lucky, to act outside the formula, but only because she has to, not because she wants to. She can't be generous about it.

Mom sort of operates on half-everything—half-steam, half-love, half-enthusiasm, etc. Certainly half-awareness.

For a time, Betsey lived with my mom, when her kids were about twelve and seven and four. We all realized that my mother favored girls, presumably because she had daughters herself and seemed to assume they were just nicer than boys. That didn't mean that she thought *we* were good kids, but that she thought,

89

in the abstract, that girls were inherently better. I remember the scorn she sometimes showed my nephews, Paul and David, when they lived with her. Once, I was sitting in the kitchen with her when Paul came in and opened the refrigerator. My mother scowled at him and shook her head, as though he had no right to get a snack, even though he was living there. She could have taken him aside and suggested that he always ask permission first. But her modus operandi was to disapprove, in that vague, nonverbal, derisive way we all knew so well. Later on, when she showed some of this disdain for my son, Doug, I would immediately interrupt her or remove Doug from the situation. She was infuriating.

I've asked Paul, now a married man, what he remembers from the time he lived with my mother. How would he describe her? He thinks for a minute and answers, "Stern." He follows up with "remote" and "detached." I ask him if he felt wounded by her. "No," he says thoughtfully. "It was as though she kept herself removed from us." It was also, I realize, that Betsey protected them from her.

In later years, when my mother had moved into the nursing home and my family had relocated to Cleveland, I attempted to visit whenever I came to town and usually brought the kids, in the hope that she would enjoy them. She didn't pay them a lot of attention, though. Sometimes she had candy that someone had brought, just the thing to make a boring visit to a nursing home more palatable to my kids. But my mother never offered them a treat. I would wait awhile, and as they grew bored and antsy, I would finally ask her if they could have something to eat. "Oh, yes!" she'd say. She seemed happy, most of the time, to see them enjoy a snack. But she never, ever offered it herself.

I ask my adult son what he remembers about Grandma Miller. He recalls her quiet voice and remembers her being in a wheelchair. He remembers the long walk through the halls of the nursing home to her room and the eager, discomfiting smiles of the other patients. Did he sense any affection from my mother? "Only because you said she liked to see us," he answers.

Do you remember any conversation with her? "She said something like, 'There isn't much for you to do here, is there?'"

Do you remember her house, before the nursing home? "Only the junk on the kitchen table."

He remembers her coming to my in-laws' house for holidays or going out to restaurants for birthdays. He remembers having to drive her back to the nursing home and feeling relieved when my sister took her back instead. He can't remember much else. She died when he was twelve.

Who knows what she was feeling all this time? I've found an Australian friend, Michael, through my blog, who cajoles, encourages, and challenges me. He says that making something real, putting emotions and thoughts into action, takes power. My mother lacked that power, and so her real thoughts and feelings stayed on the inside. We have discussed the term "curator" with respect to my husband, who programs films, and Michael says, "Your mother couldn't curate her own life."

When it came to little babies, though, I sensed some of my mother's best and most maternal instincts. When my sisters and I were born, between 1943 and 1951, experts still warned parents not to spoil their children. Dr. L. Emmett Holt's theories held sway. In 1894, his bestselling *The Care and Feeding of Children* prescribed a strict feeding schedule and warned against kissing and cuddling. He suggested that four months was a good time for toilet training. (Toilet-training in the United States now begins at around two years old.) In 1928, Dr. John B. Watson, a behaviorist, followed in Holt's footsteps, with the latest behaviorist research to back him up. His 1928 handbook *Psychological Care of Infant and Child* advised, "Never hug or kiss [your children], never let them sit in your lap . . . If you must, kiss them once on the forehead when they say goodnight. Shake hands with them in the morning." He recommended tying children's hands to the bedposts at night to cure them of thumb-sucking.

Dr. Watson's procrustean teaching still dominated when Dr. Benjamin Spock came along to shake things up. *The Common Sense Book of Baby and Child Care*, published in 1946, advised parents to trust their instincts. "You know more than you think you do," Spock sensibly suggested. He advocated flexibility in feeding schedules and toilet training and even maintained that parenting could be fulfilling and enjoyable! Cuddling and affection, he wrote, were healthy for both parents and children.

My mother, a disciple of Dr. Spock, felt that babies deserved love and affection and couldn't be spoiled. This was an appealing, softer side of my mother. There was a time, I had to imagine, when she loved us unconditionally, before her profound disillusionments, and when she herself felt needed and loved. I enjoyed hearing my mother talk about those times and her fondness for Dr. Spock, and hoped that she really did mother us in this fashion when we were babies.

My mother regarded the prospect of children's growing up as infinitely sad. Watching little ones get older makes all parents nostalgic, but my mother's attitude was typically extreme and dysfunctional, at least for me. As the youngest, I was subconsciously aware that I was continuously disappointing her by growing up. "I wish we could go back to when you all were babies," she would say. On my birthdays, she frequently said, "I wish I could keep you little forever."

But I kept growing up and growing away from her. There was nothing either of us could do to stop it, but it was clear that she wished I would always remain a little girl. I imagine this regret made it hard for her to talk to me about sex or dating. All those abandonments—graduating, going away to school, getting married—each milestone forced her to surrender, unwillingly, to the inevitable. Grandchildren must have been so disconcerting, in that she couldn't really accept that her own kids had grown up. How could her children have children? No wonder she sometimes behaved as though her grandchildren were not quite real.

Causes

People with a borderline personality disorder have grown up feeling that they are unfairly treated, that they didn't get the attention or care they needed.

John G. Gunderson, *Borderline Personality Disorder: A Clinical Guide*

I sit in the small, tidy kitchen of my grandparents' home, filled with the smell of coffee, deeper and richer than it's ever smelled since. My grandmother pours me a cup of dark coffee in a china cup and adds an unhealthy dollop of real, rich cream. She slices into warm homemade coffee cake, puts it on a plate, and covers it with sweetened, cold, juicy strawberries.

I spent afternoons like this with my grandparents as a teenager and young adult. It was my advantage as the youngest child. My sisters were grown up and gone. My mom hardly drove at all, so when my grandmother needed groceries or wanted a ride to the doctor, it often fell to me.

My grandmother, Margaret Skiffington Grimm, was a stalwart, energetic, outgoing little woman, just over five feet tall. When I think of her, the word "plucky" comes to mind. She immigrated to the United States from Ireland as a little girl in about 1890, traveling with her mother and sister to join her father, who'd moved here first. She was self-assured and had lots of lifelong friends, whom she called her chums. She kept a very neat house and loved cooking and serving food. I loved her baked goods and started my love affair with coffee when I first drank her richly brewed Maxwell House as a college student. Though I'm now a vegetarian, my mouth still waters when I recall her overcooked, buttery chicken, served with warm homemade rolls. She hugged and loved her grandchildren and enjoyed having us stay overnight.

My grandmother had left school in the seventh grade in order to work. She was sharp and capable, but not well educated. A devout, old-fashioned Catholic, she kept a picture of the Sacred

Heart on the living room wall and a statue of Mary on the piano. She loved John Kennedy because he was Catholic and "looked like a President." She didn't know much about history or current events, and my mother was always impatiently correcting her mistakes.

In contrast, my grandmother seemed appreciative of my mother. As she was dying, one of the last things I heard her say to her was, "You were a good daughter." I've often thought ruefully how nice it would have been to hear that from my mother.

My grandparents, my mom, and her younger brother lived in eastside Cleveland neighborhoods and in East Cleveland, then an up-and-coming suburb. When my parents married, they moved to Canton, because my dad had gotten a job at *The Repository.* My grandparents then followed them to Canton to be near their first grandchild, Betsey.

Pop, as we called my grandfather, was taciturn. He had worked as a lineman for the electric company in Cleveland. When I was little, his gruffness scared me, but as I got older and visited my grandparents by myself, I always felt welcomed by him. He had grown up on a farm, the child of German immigrants, and loved the acreage of his retirement home in Louisville. He cultivated a huge garden, filled with corn and other vegetables.

He became fast friends with Samantha, Marge's first 4-H sheep. Sam followed Pop around the yard like a puppy. When Sam was sold at the Stark County Fair—selling a market animal is part of the project—my grandfather was noticeably saddened. When I started raising goats for 4-H, he was free to become attached, because they didn't have to be sold at market.

My mother always resented her brother George, two years her junior, whom she regarded as my grandmother's favorite. My grandmother pinned her hopes on her fair-haired boy and pretty much ignored my mother, or so my mother maintained. When George, as an adult, visited us with his family, he and my mom exchanged pleasantries, but otherwise seemed distant.

My mother had another brother, who died in infancy. We know very little about Charley, and in fact never heard about him from my mother. Marge and I first learned of him when we took Chad as a newborn to meet his great grandparents. My grandmother rocked Chad, cooing to him. Eventually, she began crying, repeating through her tears, "Oh, my baby. My little Charley."

Talking later to my mother, we learned that little Charley had a food allergy and couldn't digest any formula available at the time. This would have been around 1917, when my mother was about six years old. My grandmother had been told that she didn't have enough milk to nurse her babies. Charley couldn't digest any food that my grandmother or his doctors provided. My mother recalled the acrid smell of the cod liver oil they tried to feed the baby.

My mother answered our questions about Charley unsentimentally. She seemed contemptuous of the attention my grandmother had paid him. She seemed not to have grieved for her little baby brother, who lived for almost a year, essentially starving to death. It was as though it had happened to someone else. After sixty years, my grandmother couldn't help crying when she held Marge's little baby boy. My mother, however, described Charley's illness and death coolly and critically.

How did my mother experience her family's ordeal at the time? While my grandmother was trying to save her baby, she would almost inevitably have neglected my mom. She talked about taking the baby to the doctor on the streetcar. Did my mother feel abandoned? If these events traumatized her as a little girl and a young woman, then she may have harbored borderline tendencies from her youth—in her adolescence, during her courtship with my Dad, and in her young marriage.

Was she already exhibiting borderline traits before my dad became sick? Or was his illness the trigger? My sisters were ten and six years old when he left home for his surgeries and treatment in New York. They don't remember what my mom was like before that time. Were her resentments and her conviction that life was unfair latent in her personality, becoming more pronounced when my dad got sick?

We know the traumatic effect his disability had on my mother. She described her married life before his illness as perfect. In typical BPD splitting, she'd had a perfect husband, perfect little children, perfect life. Then my dad got sick, and it all ended. Her premature widowhood began.

Experts are divided as to the causes of borderline personality disorder. Most describe some interaction between a biological predisposition and environmental triggers. Many people with BPD exhibit symptoms in childhood or early adulthood. Others begin to show borderline traits later in life, after some trauma or abandonment. Some writers connect BPD with post-traumatic stress disorder, because they share many of the same symptoms, such as fear of abandonment, labile emotions, and depression, and because BPD seems often to arise after a trauma, such as abuse.

Not all sufferers, however, have undergone abuse, and many seem to have had normal, loving families. Dr. Robert O. Friedel, author of *Borderline Personality Disorder Demystified: An Essential Guide for Understanding and Living with BPD*, writes movingly about his sister, Denise.

Denise had emotional difficulties literally from birth; she cried more than her siblings and was difficult to soothe. In childhood, she would attack her sisters and brothers in violent rages and break their belongings. She seemed to have begun life with a strong biological disposition toward BPD. Friedel's mother surmised that the anesthetic she had received during Denise's birth (and not for her four other children) had somehow affected Denise's brain.

Friedel himself absolves his mother of any responsibility. He writes,

> *One of my most vivid memories of my mother was the way her face would light up whenever she saw one of the family. It made me feel good to my core to be caught in the radiance of her smile and the warmth of her embrace. I would*

96

watch her bestow the same love on every member of our family... There was never any doubt: she loved us all deeply and unequivocally.

Other sources, however, might blame Mrs. Friedel for Denise's problems. The term *withholding mothers* appears everywhere in the literature; mothers who don't affirm their child's feelings, who are neglectful or clearly abusive, create the kind of trauma that results in borderline traits.

These writers blatantly blame the parents or assume that abuse or trauma has created the illness. Many connect BPD with incest and abuse, and others single out mothers. Phrases like "maternal over-involvement," "maternal inconsistency," and "pathological features of maternal personality" pop up in scholarly articles. Dr. James F. Masterson puts it like this: "The object relations theory suggests that the mother's withdrawal of her libidinal availability at the child's efforts to separate and individuate produces a development arrest at the phase of separation-individuation (rapprochement subphase)."

I'm not sure, but I think this theory is blaming the mother. Christine Ann Lawson similarly puts the blame on parents. In *Understanding the Borderline Mother,* she asserts that all people with BPD have been neglected, abused, constantly denigrated, and/or abandoned by parents and deprived of emotional support. I wonder how often such experts are taking the BPD patient's word about his or her childhood. I know from experience that people with BPD perceive reality differently. I've heard my own words, distorted and misinterpreted, thrown back at me. I've been told that I said things that I didn't say. People with BPD remember their pasts differently from others who lived it with them. Therapists and family members, it's true, must listen to and validate the feelings of the BPD patient, but they shouldn't necessarily trust all of his or her memories. Psychologists used to blame mothers for schizophrenia and autism. As I read about bad mothering, I feel defensive of my affectionate grandmother and wonder whether mothers are again getting a bad rap.

Gradually, other researchers are beginning to suggest that

BPD derives from a complex combination of genetic and environmental causes and is not due solely to bad parenting. They suspect there's a biological inclination toward the disorder. The greater the biological tendency, the slighter the environmental trigger needs to be. Sometimes the trigger is called an invalidating environment, meaning that the family lacked the emotional support the child needed, but is not exactly to blame. Most parents are doing the best they can for their children, so blaming them is not the point. Rather it's important to see the *impact* parental behavior has had on children.

In other words, if a child is born with a strong tendency toward BPD, then insensitive or merely introverted parents might trigger the child's illness. Marsha Linehan argues that parents and children are sometimes "mismatched." That is, a hypersensitive child may be born to parents who are undemonstrative by nature. In such cases, no one is at fault.

Like Dr. Linehan, I resist blaming the mother. First, I'm a mother myself, and I resent the tendency of psychiatrists, since Freud, to blame mothers. Second, I knew my grandmother as welcoming and loving: a warm soft hug with a huge jeweled brooch sticking into my cheek. Perpetually dusted with flour, she was redolent of sweet desserts and rich coffee. She also showed genuine fondness for my mother, so it's hard to blame her.

Still and all, my sisters and I would admit to observing an Irish-Catholic reserve in the family, an unease with emotion, and a proclivity toward guilt. I always noted a lot of sarcasm, veiled criticism, and blatant racism (which my mother, to her credit, eschewed) when my mother's side of the family got together. Little warmth was expressed among the adults. If my mother as a little girl felt abandoned when my grandmother's attention turned to her sick infant, it's unlikely that she communicated her fears or worries. She was very young, and sharing feelings just wasn't done at that time and in that family.

She must have felt abandoned once again when my dad got sick. My mother described marriage as a fairy tale, by which she meant a lovely, unrealistic story doomed to failure. When someone we knew got divorced, or when a husband died young, my mother would comment, "Oh, they believed in the fairy tale." She envied single women and wouldn't care, she always said, if her daughters never married. When we served as bridesmaids or planned our own weddings, my mother would inevitably warn us not to believe in fairy tales. They're doomed to end unhappily, because the fairy tale isn't real.

The Closet

The outbursts are unbearable and scary . . . the depression and darkness . . . well, you know all about it . . . I have lived with it for so long that I really don't know what normal is.

BPD Sanctuary, website

I carry our household around in my head. I am generally the one who is able to find things; I know where everything is. That's why our clutter bothers me so much. Because I am *mentally* storing all the old clothes folded in the attic, Christmas ornaments, and antique books from Betty and Rudy. All the detritus in the basement—kids' toys, John's grade-school projects, rags, empty boxes, my teaching stuff from twenty years ago. All these belongings are so ponderous, I can feel their weight in my mind. I can almost feel the strain of trying to hold my head upright.

Sometimes as I'm falling asleep, my imagination moves around our home, focusing on the junk that I wish I would get rid of during daytime hours. In this in-between time, when I'm almost asleep, the geography of my head often switches from where I live now to the house where I grew up.

On many nights, my mind wanders into the downstairs closet in the middle of our house in Canton. As you came up the back stairs from the garage, you faced this closet door. Its double door, fastened with a hook, opened outward. Dark and musty, this walk-in space reminds me of C.S. Lewis's wardrobe. Frequently-worn coats were hanging in the front, near the vacuum cleaner and some brooms.

The overhead shelf stored my dad's old hats—business hats that he no longer wore, because he didn't go to work. These were felt hats that men used to wear in the 1940s and 50s, with a grosgrain band around the crown. There was also a solid white safari hat, or so we called it, a hard hat that we used to play with. As you walked further into the darkness, you came to another rack, full of my dad's old wool coats and jackets, threadbare coats of my mother's, things no longer worn but that no one ever imagined throwing away. Creeping to the back of the closet while playing Hide and Seek, you traveled back in time. The sweetly stale smell signified the past to me.

With the closet doors closed from the inside, I would stand in almost perfect darkness. This was a spooky, ideal hiding place. But if I were looking for something, if an attachment for the vacuum cleaner had fallen to the floor, I was out of luck. I always had the sense that there was more in that closet than I even knew. It was full of stuff, and it was never cleaned out, and it was too dark to find anything.

That closet needed a light. We lived with many inconveniences in that house, much that was run-down and dirty and old-fashioned; few things were ever fixed or improved. A single light bulb would have illuminated the dark corners.

Borderline personality disorder has been that light bulb for me. Why did my mother grieve at her daughters' weddings? Why did she call us losers? Why did she sit alone by the TV drinking wine and then cry herself to sleep? Why was she missing altogether at times I needed a mother? BPD has shined a light into the murky corners of my childhood. It has explained things I never understood.

If I backed out of the closet and again faced the double door, I turned right to enter the kitchen. Then, on the left, was the dining room, which opened onto the living room. A path through the living room and into the kitchen led back to the closet again. It formed the very center of our house. For too many years, I entered into this dark place as I entered into sleep.

Part 3: Unentangling

And this, then,
is the vision of that Heaven of which
we have heard, where those who love
each other have forgiven each other,

where for that, the leaves are green,
the light a music in the air,
and all is unentangled,
and all is undismayed.

Wendell Berry, "To My Mother"

My Mother/Myself

Adult children raised by a parent with BPD or its traits likely have a hard time trusting their own perceptions, their own judgment, and their emotions, and knowing what's normal.

Kimberlee Roth, *Surviving a Borderline Parent*

After the holidays this year, I feel morose and resentful. I thought I had prepared myself to feel unappreciated and to give freely without any investment in how my gifts were received.

Does that ever work?

John has irritated me by spending an entire day reading, cover to cover, a funny film book that his sister gave to him. It's an issue in our marriage that John rarely reads a book. When we were dating, he read the books that I recommended, and we bonded over them, just as we bonded over the movies he wanted me to see. I have noted, with chagrin, these thirty years, that there was a little bait-and-switch going on. Though I have continued to see movies, even some demanding and arduous ones (*Satantango*: seven hours, black and white, Hungarian), he has read only a handful of books, most of them not the ones I yearned for him to read. For him to spend hours reading a new book—a gift from his sister, no less—when he has neglected all the masterpieces I have recommended over the years, well, it was hard to take.

My second big holiday gripe is that on Christmas Day John looked worried as he opened his big, surprise gift: tickets for a concert of music by Bernard Herrmann, the movie composer. Instead of expressing gratitude, he furrowed his brow and told me that the concert was scheduled during the Cleveland International Film Festival. God forbid he'd have to miss an evening there.

These resentments are compounded, of course, by the familiar post-Christmas letdown. All the the planning, the shopping, the cooking, and baking are finished, and it's not clear whether anyone actually noticed. The Christmas detritus lies strewn around—bags of torn Christmas wrapping, opened gifts that have not yet found their home, the odd present that needs to be re-

102

turned (where to keep it in the meantime?). The leftovers. Christmas plates and dishes. All these things on top of Christmas decorations, which feel like clutter if the house isn't otherwise pristine. They burden me.

I try to unburden myself. I don't yell. I just tell John, when he asks, what's bothering me. It does not go well. He gets defensive. At one point he tells me my feelings are "silly." Not a good idea.

I spend a day or two trying to talk and pray my way out of these feelings. The connection with my mother just complicates things. Because, here's the thing. My mother always felt like a martyr. She told us a thousand times that she felt unappreciated. Now, as I've been exploring BPD, I understand that a sufferer *never* feels loved enough and is always going to be disappointed by those she's invested in.

So, on top of the Christmas angst, I worry that I have a touch of the BPD. *Surviving a Borderline Parent* explains that though children of parents with BPD are usually normal, they're going to suffer residual effects. For example, they're going to mimic certain of their parents' feelings and behaviors. So when I start thinking like a martyr—I do, and do, and do for you people and no one appreciates it!—I have one of those "my mother/myself" moments. Are my feelings valid, or am I just being my mother?

In addition, the literature explains, children of parents with BPD are going to wonder whether their perceptions correspond to reality. They've grown up being told things that don't correspond to reality. They've grown up being told that they don't hear things accurately, that the parent never said that. They've grown up hearing that their feelings are silly.

When I was in fourth grade, I was scared witless by scary movies on TV. After school, Marge and I would occasionally watch *Dracula* and *The Wolf Man,* the old Bela Lugosi and Lon Chaney versions, and these struck my innocent self as just the creepiest things. At the Palace Theater in downtown Canton, I saw a trailer—just the *trailer*—for *The Blob* and for months afterward had trouble going to sleep, worrying that the Blob was going to come squishing into my own bedroom windows.

Here's another way fear manifested itself. For Abbie's first few years, we kept her outdoors, acceding to my mother's wishes. (Eventually, of course, Abbie made her way indoors, to my mother's displeasure.) We fed her in the evenings, and instead of stepping out in daylight to deliver her dish of food, I would procrastinate until after dark. Many nights I hesitated just inside the garage door, holding her dish, peering out into the darkness toward the doghouse. I would pause there, too frightened to run out with her food. A big forsythia bush right next to Abbie's house would metamorphose in my mind into, say, a vampire. Finally I would take a deep breath and race into the backyard as fast as I could, fling down the dish and race back, certain that I was being pursued by Dracula or one of his Ohio cousins.

Even back then, in the light of day, I knew this was ridiculous. I knew those creatures were imaginary, but after dark my fears would get the better of me. This felt like a real problem, and I wondered if anyone else suffered such terrors. One day, I resolved to confide in my mom. As she was washing the dishes one afternoon, I said, "Mom, I'm scared of monsters. I watched these movies and now I think about them in the dark, and they scare me."

My mother glanced at me disdainfully and then looked away. "That's ridiculous," she said. "There are no such things. You're just being silly."

Christine Lawson writes, "When children bring concerns to the attention of the borderline parent, they receive a response that either increases their distress or entirely dismisses their concern . . . The borderline . . . is unable to reassure and comfort the child."

My mind has been wandering back to the time when Marge discovered she was pregnant; I was seventeen. She told me the news first, along with a few of her friends. I was terrified by the thought of her telling my parents, and she couldn't imagine doing it herself. Eventually, of course, she had to. She approached my dad, alone in his room, to break the news. He assured her that they'd support her and take care of her and figure out what to do. He would break the news to my mom. Marge describes what came next as "wailing and gnashing of teeth."

As weeks went by, and Marge and my parents discussed what to do—marriage or adoption—nobody talked to me. Marge, of course, was occupied with huge decisions, and my parents probably thought they were protecting me. I overheard the ongoing wailing and gnashing, but I had no idea what was happening. I gleaned that my parents hoped that Marge wouldn't get married, because they felt a good marriage wasn't based on a pregnancy.

Then Marge disappeared. She was gone, and I didn't know where she went. A few days went by, and I asked my mother. "She's gone. They got married," she responded curtly.

"Is she coming back?"

My mother shrugged impatiently. "I don't know," she said.

I felt, once again, that I shouldn't ask any more questions. I wasn't angry or grief-stricken or worried. I was, again, merely bewildered. Everyone seemed to assume that I didn't have feelings about what was going on, so I tried to oblige. I suppressed and ignored them when they arose.

A few months went by. Then one day Marge called.

"I'm in the hospital. It's a girl. She's premature and she's in an incubator, but she's okay," she said.

"Do you want to talk to Mom?" I answered.

Years later, Marge told me that my curt response had been hurtful. Certainly I now understand the effect my brusqueness had on Marge. But I also know that then I was numb and confused. I had no idea how to respond to her, and so I didn't.

I knew that if I had pressed my mom for answers, if I had tried to express my fears and concerns, if I had cried and told her that I missed my sister, I would have been told that my feelings were inconsequential compared to hers. *She* was the one who was suffering. I might well have been told I was silly. I had learned it wasn't safe to talk to my mom.

Back to today. When John says my feelings are silly, how do I know whether he's just feeling defensive and doesn't want to deal with them, or if he's right? How do I know that I'm not a bottomless pit of need like my mom? How do I know if I'm still as irrational as when one of my worst fears was a phantasmagorical vampire? More important, perhaps, how do I know that my frustration with John, when he uses the loaded word *silly*, isn't just residual anger at my mother?

Soon, he apologizes, because he is, after all, not my mother. Feeling a little better, I go for a long walk. I want to rid myself of these roiling contradictions. But before I can hope to shed them, I must first accept them and examine them. Unraveling the mystery of my mom is not so much about my mom, as it turns out, but about me instead. "Remember that writing is translation," wrote E.B. White in a letter to a young writer, "and the opus to be translated is yourself."

Parenting

I knew my mother's limitations because they formed the marrow of my bones.

Alice Sebold, *The Almost Moon*

When my daughter moved to New York City, neither John nor I offered at first to go with her, because Margaret is extraordinarily independent. Then, after discussing it, we offered to go along. To my surprise, our self-reliant daughter welcomed our help, and because John was working, I accompanied her to the big city. As we drove many hours from Cleveland, as our car overheated in Manhattan traffic, and as we shopped in a brand-new, crowded IKEA store in Brooklyn, I remained cheerful and supportive. When I saw her new apartment, I commented on its spaciousness and big windows and airiness. All this time, I carried with me the following memory.

When I decided to move from home to the Kent State campus in my junior year, I did it all alone. In fact, three years earlier, I had applied, visited, and explored colleges all on my own. During the time I lived in Kent, about half an hour from Canton, my mother visited only twice, when Marge drove her to see me. Both times, she looked around the rooms with a vague smile on her face, saying very little. In the days and weeks that followed, she had one comment on her visits: "All I felt when I was at your place was that I couldn't trust you." She was intimating that I was promiscuous. She was saying I was a bad girl.

In Margaret's New York apartment, I self-consciously avoided saying anything remotely resembling that remark.

Back when I comforted Margaret at the funeral of our goldfish, I was partly doing what came naturally, but I was also playing a part. I was deliberately trying to behave like a good mother. I was thinking, "OK, this is how you do it." I remember feeling a few moments of satisfaction: "There. You've done this one thing right."

I carry with me always my mother's example as a parent. When my kids were young and I went into the occasional rage about the messiness of our house or took on the aura of a martyr, I felt my mom's specter hovering nearby. Even now, the clutter and the disheveled state of our yard bring up ghosts. Our weedy, overgrown backyard makes me feel as I did when I was a kid. I worry that the neighborhood is noticing the disarray. I feel criticized. I feel disapproval.

Unopened mail and newspapers scattered around evoke the disordered home where I grew up. When I finish a task, when I trim the hedge or wash the kitchen floor, I feel a special and peculiar satisfaction. "Well," I think, "at least I've done that. I've washed a floor. I've thrown away some junk mail. I've scrubbed the bathtub." It will always seem to me that I've accomplished something out of the ordinary.

People often say that when you have your own kids you feel more compassion for your parents. Perhaps. I certainly understand how my mom could feel overwhelmed at times. I understand the intensity of maternal feelings. But more often her example has worked the opposite way: since becoming a parent, I've found her erratic and hurtful behavior even more mysterious. Can I imagine, in my wildest dreams, calling Margaret a slut?

Once, when I was little, my mom was trying to comb the tangles from my hair after a bath. Her frustration grew and grew until she finally grabbed my hair with her hands and shook my head back and forth with a low guttural scream. Can I empathize with her frustration? Can I imagine pulling my child's hair, frightening and hurting her in the process? Yes, I can. What I cannot imagine is simply stopping, taking a breath, and continuing. I would have apologized and hugged my child if I had done such a thing.

Some maternal instinct has carried me through, but I've also been emotionally tone deaf. Sometimes when my kids have needed me, I've felt numb and uncertain and inept. "Shit. What do I do with this?" I wonder. Should I leave them alone? Should I step in? Should I hug them? I didn't do a great job explaining sex. I freaked out when Margaret experimented with drinking and stayed out late. I spent too much time being sullen and feeling put upon and taking naps when the kids were young. I just had to get away sometimes. I was simply flummoxed a good deal of the time. Occasionally, I fear, I've been absent. My sisters and I neglect one another. We miss birthdays. We generally assume that the others are getting along fine. We rarely call. We almost never check in.

You may respond, "Well, relationships don't come with a manual, and we've all been there. None of us always knows how to respond to our kids." Many of us, I suppose, fall out of touch with relatives. I know that's true, but along the way I have felt as if I was forging new ground. Even now, hoping to respond appropriately to my grown-up kids, I find myself *imagining* what a good mother would do.

Of course, I did have another role model. Like my mom, my dad wasn't overtly affectionate. He didn't comfort us about the death of Snap. He wasn't cuddly. I can't remember his saying "I love you." When he drank too much beer, his slurred speech embarrassed me. But he was connected; he engaged with us. I'll let the anecdotes tell it.

I was a picky eater as a kid. This trait singled me out; my adventurous sisters were willing to try anything. My mother went out of her way to prepare plain meals for me, but chastised me and fussed about my diet. "You can't live your life without eating eggs," she would declare. Nevertheless, I got attention. I was unique. No matter that the attention was negative.

Her solution to my persnickety palate was to put a small serving of the vegetables I disliked on my plate. I suppose this seemed a reasonable way to get me to try them. But for me, the sight and smell of those peas, overcooked asparagus, or beans ruined the meal. Eventually, I would force that forkful into my mouth and sometimes hold it in my cheek endlessly, because I couldn't swallow it. When I tried to force down the vegetables, I would gag.

I can imagine, now, how infuriating my behavior must have been. Much ado about nothing. Such small bites! At the time, I felt guilty. I didn't know what was wrong with me. Why didn't I like the foods that everyone else ate? My mother acted as though my refusal to eat was just to spite her. Being a good mother meant feeding your children properly, and I was making that impossible.

Once I held a piece of asparagus in my cheek until I couldn't stand it anymore. I excused myself and went to the bathroom to flush it down the toilet. When I returned to the table, my mother asked me if that's what I had done, and I denied it. At bedtime, overwhelmed with guilt, I admitted that I'd lied. My mother told me solemnly that as a result of my lying she could never trust me again.

My dad, in contrast, tried to understand. One evening during dinner, my mother was complaining about all the foods I wouldn't eat. "How is she going to live?" she asked, as though I weren't there. "Why does she do this to me? I try. I cook things for her and she just refuses to eat them."

My dad lost patience. "Look at her, Eleanore," he said. "Does she look happy? Don't you think she would try those things if she could? I think maybe kids are more sensitive to taste than adults."

He turned to me. "Do you wish you liked to eat more foods?" he asked, and I silently nodded.

Then he told my mom, "She really doesn't like vegetables. I believe she would eat them if she could." I was amazed that I was being defended.

When I had to read *The Great Gatsby* in high school, my dad read it along with me. At that stage of my life, the novel left me cold. I barely followed the plot and had no clue what it was supposed to be about. My dad remarked that Gatsby was a gangster (news to me) and said that the book was about the American Dream. I was impressed that he was so smart, and his respect for the book prepared me to love it when I was ready, a few years later.

When we kids received books as gifts, or when we loved particular books, my dad often read them, too. He thought that *Charlotte's Web,* my all-time favorite book, was funny, which it is, but I didn't realize it when I was little. He found *The Catcher in the Rye* funny, too, while also objecting to the bad language. Since his own cursing never extended beyond *damn* and *hell,* the novel's stronger language offended him, but his appreciation for a book I loved so much meant a great deal to me.

It's sad, but true. I cannot remember my mother ever reading one of our books, or any book. Although we had shelves filled with books, and both my parents espoused reading, and my mom had a degree in history and had, it seemed, read a lot in the past, she never actually read an entire book that I can recall. When she had one in hand—she requested Gloria Vanderbilt's memoir from the library, for instance—I remember thinking this is good, this is healthy; she's going to read a book. But she didn't. She leafed through it instead, and looked at the index to select certain passages. It was as though she couldn't commit herself to an entire book. She could read only passages, only magazine articles, only parts of wholes. A whole book would demand attending to it. To read a book from start to finish was to engage, and she hung back, unwilling to commit. This seems strange to me because reading was valued so highly in my house. Books were everywhere. I couldn't understand why my mother didn't read them.

When I had poems published in my high school and college literary magazines, my dad read them. He seemed skeptical, because poetry was not really his thing, but he read them and expressed his admiration nonetheless. When I started listening to classical music, he claimed not to understand, but was intrigued that I liked it. He drove us to Blossom Music Center during its first season to hear the Cleveland Orchestra play Beethoven's Fifth Symphony, which I had performed with my high-school band.

A myriad of pleasant little memories. My dad occasionally petted the dog, so hated by my mother. Abbie entertained him. When she was tied outside, she'd circle around her doghouse until she was immobilized. My dad sat at the window and watched her untangle herself, circling around backwards until she had the full length of chain again and could move around more freely. "She's pretty smart," he marveled. He allowed the cat to sleep on his lap. I remember sitting on my dad's lap myself to watch TV. I remember kissing his bristly cheek when I went to bed.

He told us stories of the times he had spent on the boats of Lake Erie, earning enough money for college. He recounted stories of his trip out West, driving his eccentric and rich Aunt Bessie and Uncle Charley. These stories were funny and also had moral lessons, of course. My mother rarely told stories, and when she did, they seemed to put someone else, like her brother or her mother, in a bad light.

Dad showed an interest. When I became infatuated with my third-grade teacher, Mrs. Define, I quoted her constantly. As soon as I got home from school, my amused father would ask, "What did Mrs. Define say today?" Once, the same year, my friend Bobby Palmer responded, "That's an insultment" to something I had said, and that locution pleased my dad endlessly. He would often respond haughtily to criticism: "That's an insultment."

He typed my term papers for me. I hated doing it myself. Inevitably, in those ancient days of typewriters, I'd reach the bottom of the page, discover I'd left no room for footnotes, and realize with despair that I'd have to retype the whole page. My dad, whose hunt-and-peck method was remarkably fast, typed papers for me, copying my messy manuscript.

He taught my sisters to drive. He was hospitalized in New York when I was learning, so couldn't teach me, but I remember much of his advice. I always scrape the snow off my headlights, I never pass trucks on a hill, and in snowy weather I turn the steering wheel *into* a skid. My mom played no part in my driving instruction.

Two doors down from our house was Willow Springs Swim Club, where my sisters worked and where I took lessons from an early age. I used to beg my mom to come swimming with me sometime, but she never did. One day, my dad drove our old Plymouth to the pool and parked outside the chain-link fence to watch me swim. He couldn't come into the pool area with his wheelchair, but he did the best he could, leaning out the car window to see me.

Driving with his hand controls was one of the ways my dad showed his independence and also took some of the driving burden off my mom's shoulders. Once, in high school, when I was in a music contest far out of town, my dad drove me there so that my mom wouldn't have to. Unable to come in to the school building and not wanting to trouble me with handling the wheelchair, he sat in the car the whole day, eight hours or so, waiting for me. At the time, distracted by nervousness over my performance, I felt only vaguely appreciative of my dad's gesture. Now, I imagine him sitting alone all day in a car, listening to the radio, reading and thinking and waiting, and I belatedly feel grateful.

When I was in college, still living at home, I would sometimes drive home by way of a small city park and stop there to take a walk. One time, I was alone in a wooded area, returning to the car. I looked up to see a man, pale and fleshy, standing nearby, studying me with a slight smile. He said hello and began walking beside me. I went on alert. I could feel the hairs on the back of my neck. I was intent on one goal: getting out of the park and into my car, alone.

The man made small talk as he walked beside me. We came to a little stream, and as we stepped across, he grasped my hand.

112

When we had crossed the stream and I tried to pull away, he held on tighter. Finally, he let go, and said with a smile, "I'm not going to hurt you."

We were now out of the woods and in a small grassy area. The car was in sight. I walked faster, turned to him and said good bye and quickly entered my car.

My heart was pounding as I drove away. I realized I had left my car unlocked, with my books and notebooks lying on the seat; some of them contained my phone number and address. I worried about his having gotten that information before he found me in the park.

When I got home, still flushed and shaken, I described to my parents what had happened. My dad furrowed his brow and shook his head. He said, "Oh, Kathy, you have to be careful."

Then he said, "He didn't hurt you, did he?" No, no, I said. It really wasn't anything. I told you all of it. He shook his head, looking worried, and told me again I had to be careful. I noted—*I felt*—his concern. My mother looked away and said nothing.

When I began dating my husband, I carried with me all that I had learned from my parents. I had lived alone with my mother for several years, when I wasn't at school. My love for my dad was buried deep under the layers of guilt I felt about his death. My expectations of parents came mostly from my mother.

I steered clear of John's parents, Dee and Stan, as much as possible. They belonged to a country club. They were Republicans. I believed we had nothing in common. When I had to interact with them, I almost hid behind John. Always shy to begin with, I assumed they wouldn't like me and figured their politeness veiled their true feelings.

As I got to know them over many years, I discovered that they indeed had faults, like everyone else. Dee could be intrusive, and Stan sometimes displayed a temper. I heard family members exchange harsh words and watched as they harbored resentments. Still, I gradually came to regard Stan and Dee as good parents of a classic all-American sort. Solid and dependable, John's dad ran a successful car dealership. Dee was the stereotypical, nurturing stay-at-home mom. John's boyhood friend, Joel, told me this story about her. One Saturday morning, very early, when they were kids, Joel knocked on the Ewings' back door. When he came in the house, Dee was wearing an apron, baking chocolate-chip cookies, and singing, "Oh, What a Beautiful Morning" from *Oklahoma*.

From my perspective, John had an idyllic childhood. He grew up in an affluent neighborhood where he rode bikes with his friends and his mom helped him organize the annual Peanuts Club carnival, inspired by the comic strip. She was a room mother for his classes at school and created her children's Halloween costumes. I remember John telling me once that he knew he could always go home. He was confident that no matter what kind of trouble he got into, his parents would always take him in. His assurance startled me. What must it be like to be so confident of your parents' love? What must it have been like to have a mother so involved in your life?

When we told John's parents we were getting married, they weren't surprised. They thought we had a lot in common and that our different religious backgrounds (me Catholic, John a Methodist) no longer presented the problem they once might have. No doubt, as parents, they had concerns, but they showed us their confidence and support. My mother, as I've said, told me that John would forever remind her of how much I'd disappointed her.

I continued to learn how different from my mom John's parents were. When John and I returned from our Seattle honeymoon, which included a week-long side trip to Alaska (a generous wedding gift from his parents), they helped us move into our first apartment, a 4th-floor walk-up. In their late fifties at the time, they gamely hauled boxes and furniture up all those stairs on a hot July day. Of course, my mom couldn't physically have helped with this arduous work. What startled me was that Stan and Dee did it all graciously, without harsh words or any mention of how much we owed them.

Soon after, my mother-in-law said she wanted to help me decorate our apartment. I wasn't sure what she meant. It wasn't Christmas, so what were we decorating? She measured the windows in our apartment and then took me to an old Canton furniture store called Thurin's and purchased valences, curtains, and curtain rods for all our windows. We trudged up all those stairs with our purchases and together cheerfully installed all the rods and hung the curtains after a quick pressing. Our apartment looked homey and more finished.

When Doug was born a few years later, Dee offered to stay with us. My mother didn't call or write a note. She just waited in the kitchen until I could visit her. I couldn't imagine what Dee and I would do all day. Sit around talking? Because we had no extra bedroom, she agreed not to stay overnight, but insisted on bringing dinner. I thought, I can walk around. I can cook. John said, "She really wants to. Let her do it." Okay, I sighed. She can bring something.

That evening, Dee and Stan arrived with a huge picnic basket. It contained a giant plate of hot fried chicken, four steaming baked potatoes, green beans, and a salad. The piece de resistance was a homemade chocolate layer cake, John's favorite, and okay by me, too. She had packed napkins and plates and plastic ware, so that there would be no cleanup. It was like watching Mary Poppins unpack her suitcase. I sat down, ate, and felt cared for.

When Dee died of a sudden heart attack at the age of seventy, I lost someone I loved and someone who loved me, and maybe more importantly, someone who dearly loved my children. I try to believe that my mother loved me, because, after all, that's what mothers do. I remember feeling loved when I was very small, when I followed her around the house and thought she was pretty and begged her to come to the swimming pool with me. But as a teenager and adult, I didn't *feel* loved. Friends and acquaintances demur if I'm ever so tactless as to say this out loud. They respond automatically, "Oh, no, I'm sure she loved you." But I have never been sure.

I ask my sisters this question: Did our mother love us? Marge replies that she can't think of a time she felt loved by her. Betsey sends this email: "I've been mulling your query. I believe that the answer is yes. But I think that she was so wrapped up in her own pain that she didn't display her love well. Upon reading that last sentence, I also think that it's something of an understatement!"

If she didn't love us, or didn't show it, it must have been because she couldn't. "Although she can function extraordinarily well in other roles," writes Christine Lawson, "mothering is the single most daunting task for the borderline female. Her fear of abandonment and her tendency to experience separation as rejection or betrayal lock the borderline mother and her children in a struggle for survival. The child is emotionally imprisoned. Children must separate to survive, but separation threatens their mother's survival."

So none of us saw her love "displayed." We didn't feel supported or forgiven, cherished or respected. I commented in my journals soon after my father died that my mother never seemed to *notice* me, except when she was angry with me. It hurts me to realize that she never really knew me. This is why my mother-in-law's love was such an amazing, unexpected gift. Like my dad, she taught me that loving gestures, engagement, and interest make a difference in other people's lives, especially in children's lives.

John grieved, of course, when his mother died. He was sad but not devastated. He told me, "Well, she loved me, and I knew it. I loved her, and she knew that, too." It was so straightforward and so simple. I tried to take it in.

Fifteen years or so after my mother's death, I was talking with friends about our birthdays. One friend admitted feeling hurt when her grown kids didn't call her with birthday greetings until very late at night, almost as an afterthought. Another friend said, "Well, of course, it's unthinkable that we mothers would forget *their* birthdays."

I spoke up about my mother, hesitant, as always, and afraid of sounding bitter. "I can remember the first birthday my mother didn't notice," I said. "I was in my twenties. My birthday came and went, with no card and no phone call. I visited her on the following weekend and waited for her to mention it. Finally I said, 'You know my birthday was this week?' She smiled pleasantly and said, 'Oh, yes. How was it?'"

I stopped there, but I recalled feeling at that moment that I was in a new place. I didn't chastise her. I just reconciled myself, once again, to more limited expectations. There were times after that when we celebrated together, when we had a family get-to-gether, but she never sent me a card or called me. She never went out, never shopped, never bought cards, never called.

My friends seemed surprised. They asked why my mother would have ignored my birthday. Was she angry? No, I said. Not exactly.

"Dementia?" one said.

No, no, I answered. How could I explain? "It was just her," I said.

But I do know, now. She was incapable of dealing with other people and the emotions that relationships evoked. Beyond that, she had a profound sense of her own unimportance. She thought that nothing she did mattered, so why should she do anything? I could go on recounting instances where my dad, and later my in-laws, made a positive difference to me. But my mom was con-vinced she had no effect on anyone. No effect on us.

I gradually began to understand my mother's sense of emp-tiness and helplessness by listening to my friend Nancy, who told me that when she leaves a social gathering, she senses that she has disappeared. When I asked her to explain, she told me, "I don't matter." When she's alone, she feels that she's unreal to other people, and when they leave her, they are impalpable, alto-gether gone. A BPD blogger who calls himself "geordieger" puts it like this: "Only last year I realized that when a person left a room they didn't just 'disappear' into a void. I couldn't understand how someone could still be there when I couldn't see them."

I compare this way of thinking to my own. In my mind, I imagine the people who aren't with me. I think of Marge, and I imagine her at her farm petting her dogs or feeding her horses. When I think of John throughout the day, I picture him at work interacting with his coworkers or typing on his computer. I imag-ine Margaret shopping in New York or hanging out in her apart-ment, and Doug at his job or in his car. Now I believe that my mother couldn't do this. Her mind didn't work this way. When we weren't physically with her, it was as though we didn't exist. We weren't anywhere. From her point of view, we had vanished.

My mother never tried to connect to me and my sisters. When we weren't with her, we weren't real. When we were with her, we were always just about to abandon her again.

Unentangling

I can be changed by what happens to me. But I refuse to be reduced by it.

Maya Angelou

If asked, at her last conscious moment, my mother would have said she was unhappy living in the nursing home. She didn't want to participate in the activities there, she wanted to go home, her fairy-tale life had been ruined when her husband got sick, she had no money, and, oh yeah, her daughters had disappointed her. As far as I know, she was unhappy up to that final moment, when she fell asleep for the last time, unable to fight off the pneumonia that ended her life. Dr. James F. Masterson has written of borderline patients, "They lack the essential capacities to enjoy their lives." My mother's misery crouches in my consciousness, hiding, waiting to be called out. And when it wants to be felt, there it is.

I always wished I could alleviate my mother's pain. When I was very young, I would crawl into bed with her when I heard her crying at night. Then, when I was ten, I realized she was angry at Betsey, and then, soon after, at Marge. I believed, at least in part, that they were *making* her unhappy. They were mostly out of the house by that time, and I was left at home listening to my mother's laments. I wanted my listening to help her.

In 1967, during my sophomore year in high school, when Betsey got married and Marge was living on her own, when my dad was flown to New York for surgery and months of therapy, there we were, my mom and me—alone in the house. She was feeling desperate about the betrayal of her older daughters, their abandonment, or their just growing up. My dad was gone. She had no friends. Who besides me did she have to talk to?

Fifteen years old, I listened to my mom and tried to respond. I was confused about the choices my sisters had made, but I knew that in moving out and finding boyfriends, they were behaving normally. I loved them, and I knew my mother wasn't easy to live with. The cloud of gloom and all that. No wonder they moved away.

At the same time, I noticed that my mother seemed cheerful around other people. When Betty and Rudy visited, she smiled and conversed and never betrayed her bitterness. At church, she was cordial, if distant, and later on in the nursing homes, the staff always told me and my sisters how pleasant and cooperative my mother was. We would exchange knowing and frustrated looks. Why did she save all of her bitterness and cutting remarks for us?

In Augusten Burroughs's memoir *A Wolf at the Table,* he writes this about his dad: "I remembered thinking how, in the light of day out in the world, my father was just like anybody's father. But as soon as I was alone with him again, *Dad* was gone and *dead* was there in his place. . . I realized my father was two men—one he presented to the outside world, and one, far darker, that was always there, behind the face everybody else saw." My mother, like Burroughs's father, showed us her darker face and saved the happy one for others.

Much of the time, in later years, I was impatient with my mother. Her predictable pessimism drove me crazy. I always anticipated what she was going to say about the weather, her loneliness, and the dog. I would snap at her in response. I was not a model daughter. That's why I was so taken aback when she insisted I had always been perfect. I thought, "Me? I'm not even nice to you half the time."

As years went by, I felt more and more estranged from her. At the same time, I wanted to understand her. Most of all, I wanted her to be happier. I wanted her to drive again. I wanted her to go to a church social event or meeting, anywhere, just to get out of the house. I wanted her to make the occasional phone call. I wanted her to stop being so passive. I wanted her to fix up her house—to call the repairman and the plumber and not procrastinate and wait for one of us to do it for her. I urged her, over and over, to do these things, but to no effect. The word *crazy* may have crossed my mind when I was impatient with her, but I never seriously considered that she was mentally ill and certainly never took in all that it might mean.

Haplessly, I even tried to arrange friendships for her. Ruth, a fellow teacher of mine, was married to a man disabled by multiple sclerosis, and Ruth felt burdened by caring for him. Perfect, I thought. They both have had a handicapped spouse, and they've both dealt with MS. They can become friends and have someone to confide in, someone who will really know how they feel. Someone, I couldn't help thinking, who will take my mother's focus off me. When they met for lunch, the desultory conversation consisted mainly of complaints. Afterwards, my mom showed no interest in seeing Ruth again, although she felt sorry for her. Ruth, in turn, felt sorry for my mom. She regretted that, since she had her hands full with her husband, she couldn't take on my mom. Where I was hoping for mutual support and sharing, they saw each other as another burden.

I felt that burden myself. Once, after I was married, I told my mom that my life was pretty good, except for just one thing. My only serious problem, I said, was my mother. I said that her unhappiness troubled me more than anything else in my life. I expected her to be horrified to hear that she was her daughter's worst problem. I expected her to change. What I was saying was so dramatic, so overwhelming, and so true, it was bound to make a difference.

Instead, she had an eerily familiar reaction. I saw the same look pass over her face as when I asked her to stop saying my dad was ashamed of me—that cryptic expression resembling satisfaction. Only now, years later, am I beginning to understand. She wanted more than anything to communicate her unhappiness, and in that moment I affirmed her deepest emotion. For one moment, she could feel that for once someone understood her misery.

My friend Nancy has made great progress, working with a compatible therapist and sticking with her. By its very nature, BPD makes therapy hard. "The work of therapy," says therapist Lauren Slater in *Welcome to My Country*, ". . . is the work of relationship." Because borderline patients, by definition, have trouble with relationships, they have trouble with therapy. Their therapists inevitably disappoint them, they get angry, and they quit. (To say nothing of the occasional therapist who blames the BPD patient for not getting better.)

Nancy has persevered despite the vagaries of insurance coverage, her intermittent disappointment in her therapist, and, most challenging of all, her own pessimism. Nancy has made substantive changes in her life and her thinking. As she has become aware of her borderline traits, they have gradually diminished.

In the past, when she was unhappy, nothing in her life was right. She was perpetually worried about money, her job, and her relationships. She frequently chose me to be the one to hear these things. After one lengthy and agonizing phone conversation, I went upstairs to our bedroom, sat on the bed, and cried. For the first time, I realized how familiar my feelings were. My tears were not only about Nancy, but also about something very old and deep inside. I was taking on her unhappiness. Beyond that, I was piling it on top of my mother's, which I seemed to have carted around inside me unawares.

How long had I been doing this? Perhaps since I lay in bed, listening to my mother cry herself to sleep in the next room.

It was another epiphany. All those feelings, right under the surface. The gloom that Betsey talked about, hanging over our home. I had dragged it along and carried it around with me like a blanket.

In my own mind, I resolved simply to validate Nancy's feelings from then on and to stop trying to convince her of anything, to stop trying to change her or even make her feel better. It had never gotten us anywhere, and what she needed most was love and reassurance. I would not be pulled into talking about her other relationships.

But she calls, and there it is—the old pattern. The intractable gloom, the determined misery. I feel the familiar sinking in my stomach. I point out how well she's doing. She's making more money, she's improved her work situation, she's in therapy, and so on, and so on. I fend her off with positive responses; I have to, just to keep from being swept into the vortex of her despair. She listens appreciatively, and I warm to my topic. I'm having insights. I can help. I know I can say some things to help her.

Just like the old pep talks with my mom. Let's go for a drive. Want to go out to lunch? How about going to the grocery store with me? My mother adamantly refused, sometimes pleasantly. Sometimes, if an argument ensued, she would say that nobody ever understood or appreciated her. Why, she would ask, is she always the one who's wrong? Finally, I would get it, as I had before, dozens of previous times. I could talk and explain and suggest, but I couldn't budge the pain, that boulder of immovable resentment and fear. What I wish I could have said was, "I care about you. I'm sorry things are so hard." My insights and well-crafted arguments never did any good.

Likewise with Nancy: I'm slow to give up. I argue with her feelings instead of acknowledging them. I tell her how to be. When that doesn't work, I blame her at first and then begin to get it. I think to myself, "I'm a slow learner," and I tell my husband, "There's something wrong with me." Why do I continue to make the same mistake over and over again? Why do I always think that if I say the right thing I can make things better?

One night, I lie in bed, unable to sleep. I get up and watch TV, and my husband comes downstairs to check on me. When I try to explain, I start to cry, tell him thanks for asking, and send him back upstairs.

The connections slowly continue to be made. "Codependents," Melody Beattie writes in *Codependent No More*, "think they know best how things should turn out and how people should behave." They "feel responsible for other people." They "eventually fail in their efforts" and become "frustrated and angry." Has Melody Beattie met me?

I may learn slowly, but, still, I am learning. Though I can be there for Nancy, I can't make things better. I can't fix her life. I'm starting to understand, and as I work backwards from this realization, there's another epiphany. If I can't fix things for Nancy, then maybe I could never have fixed them for my mother either. This seems so obvious that surely everyone else on earth would have realized it before me. But everyone hasn't always realized. My mother's doctor once urged me to visit her more often, when she complained to him of neglect. My friend Bob, the house-painter, admonished me to take her out now and then, not realizing that it would have taken explosives to get her out of the kitchen. It seems I had some reinforcement—not least from my mother herself—in believing that her unhappiness was my fault.

Now, with two decades' perspective since my mom died and with the wisdom of the ages, along with pop psychology, I'm getting it. Every source, from the Twelve Steps to Dr. Phil to my very wise pastor, emphasizes that you can never fix another person. You can fix only yourself. I have also known, for many years, the definition of the word "codependent." My husband used to tell me, "Kathy, you're not going to change her." Those words always glanced off me. I couldn't take them in. It's true: I could have been nicer. I wish I hadn't been resentful and sarcastic. But those were my inappropriate, defensive reactions to her. Even I never truly believed that my disrespectful attitudes or dating a divorced guy caused her unhappiness.

At the same time, deep down, that's exactly what I've always believed.

In all my reading about borderline personality disorder, I have become a fan of Marsha Linehan's dialectical behavior therapy, a cumbersome name for a powerful idea. While Dr. Linehan was treating patients who attempted suicide and who self-harmed by cutting or other means, she also studied Eastern philosophy and was beginning her own meditation practice. Eureka! In dialectical behavior therapy, she brought dialectics together with Zen to treat borderline patients. Zen has to do with finding balance, and how many hundreds of times did I yearn for balance when I was talking to my mom? All my admonitions were attempts to balance the scale: things aren't all bad, look at the bright side, everything isn't horrible.

Dialectics, in philosophy, has to do with logical argumentation in the pursuit of truth. Its goal is not necessarily winning an argument, but arriving at a consensus. With synthesis as the goal, each party has to concede that the other side might contain some truth.

Instead of contradicting the borderline's thought patterns, dialectical therapy directly acknowledges BPD's all-or-nothing thinking. It guides patients toward a gradual acceptance of opposites. Dialectical therapist Andrea Bloomgarden explains it this way:

Usually people with BPD cannot conceive of being angry and loving toward the same person in the same moment. Similarly, they cannot imagine accepting themselves exactly as they are and viewing their "dysfunctional" behaviors as actually containing a bit of wisdom and functionality. When a person with BPD can truly embrace opposite concepts, ideas, and feelings in the same moment, a synthesis has occurred, and in this synthesis is the basis of healing from the disorder.

"I'm always wrong," my mom used to say. No, no, I would respond. It's not that you're wrong, exactly. It's that you're hurting yourself. It's that your perspective seems out of whack. It's that you see the damn glass as half-empty all the damn time. Dr. Phil would have asked her, "How is this working for you?"

Yet saying such things to people with BPD is tantamount to telling them they're *always* wrong. Pointing out a flaw in their thinking is telling them that they themselves are totally flawed. They're inclined to believe they're worthless anyway, and their particular turn of mind requires one or the other: right or wrong. The genius of dialectical behavior therapy is assuring patients they're often right. It assumes that patients have some insight into their own life. Their choices may not work out well, but they have an internal logic. They make some kind of sense. "The goal," says Bloomgarden, "is to help the person find that wisdom."

In order to do this, both the therapist and patient must confront paradox. The patient has to feel unconditionally accepted and commit herself to change at the same time. Ordinarily, when you tell a person with BPD she has to change, she hears that she's unacceptable. In this therapy's brilliant insight, both the patient and therapist, up front and throughout therapy, openly acknowledge the inherent contradiction in what they're doing. As the title of the off-Broadway musical would have it, "I Love You, You're Perfect, Now Change." Bloomgarden writes, "This too is an example of embracing of opposites. One can recognize the need to stay the same, to accept oneself exactly as is, and also the need to change."

This nuanced perspective reminds me of Mary Doria Russell's first two novels, *The Sparrow* and *Children of God*, science-fiction accounts of interplanetary travel, religion, and culture. In the first, a priest named Emilio has returned to Earth after a visit to another planet, suffering from post-traumatic stress disorder. I won't ruin the ending of this very suspenseful book, but by the end we learn that he has suffered grueling, sustained torture in that other world. In the sequel, Russell sets herself a tough challenge: telling the same story from the point of view of the torturers. In an interview, she describes her goal in the second book as making her readers cry when one of those torturers died. That is, she wants to turn our sympathies so completely that we grieve for someone we know, in another context, as a villain.

Balance, shades of gray, paradox, being a little bit right and a little bit wrong. "Everyone has his reasons," says a character in Jean Renoir's 1939 film *The Rules of the Game*. There are usually many more than two sides to every story. Complexity and contradiction are problematic for everyone. They're especially challenging for people with BPD.

Marsha Linehan and DBT have a little wisdom to offer me, too, since I need to be fixing (or at least working on) myself rather than someone else. If opposites are real but not mutually exclusive, as Zen would have it, then you can be right and wrong at the same time. A friend can be well-meaning and also codependent. A good daughter can screw up. A nice Catholic girl might date a divorced guy, an intelligent and responsible young woman might flunk out of college, and a man with a disability can be a worthy and capable husband and father. If all those things are true, and I believe they are, then maybe my mother also embodied some contradictory truths. Maybe I can quit choosing up sides. Maybe I can quit trying to fix her in retrospect. Maybe I can stop insisting she was wrong and I was right. Maybe I can embrace opposites.

I have certain fond memories of my mom, and I admired her in certain ways. A feminist, my mother convinced her daughters we were as smart as anyone else and that education was important. She made clear that a woman's value wasn't defined by marriage or looks. She helped mold me in positive ways. I compose a list for dialectical purposes. Here are a few items on the positive side of the ledger. These are matters that I always felt proud of—the pleasant, admirable, and interesting sides to my mom.

- She earned a Master's degree in history from Columbia University in 1935. She wrote her dissertation on the French Revolution. The degree was framed on her bedroom wall during my childhood.
- My mother could recite passages from Longfellow and the English Romantics. She had read *Ivanhoe,* a book I've never read but which has an old-fashioned, romantic allure to me.
- My mother loved Bing Crosby. She said she married my father because he could whistle almost as well. She also loved Rudy Vallee and thought Leslie Howard and Eddie Arnold were handsome.
- Throughout the late fifties and sixties, my mother ironed her three daughters' white long-sleeved Oxford shirts every week. Sometimes we were embarrassed by the odor of her cigarette smoke in our clothes, but we continued to wear those pressed blouses.
- My mother made dinner for the five of us every night. We always ate our evening meal together. It consisted of meat, potatoes, and a vegetable, except when she made a casserole. Casseroles included kidney stew and stuffed

peppers, which she had learned to make during World War II, when meat was rationed.

- My mother disagreed sharply with her own mother on the issue of race. When my grandmother made racist remarks, my mother always rebuked her.
- My mother was accepting of homosexuality.
- My mother taught me to embroider French knots.
- My mother helped me finish sewing my gathered skirt for my seventh-grade home economics class.
- My mother never criticized my appearance.
- She often woke me in the morning by singing "K-K-K-Katy, Beautiful Katy."
- My mother completed the *Saturday Review* Double-Crostic, along with my dad, every week.
- My mother told us how in 1939 Eleanor Roosevelt intervened to permit the African-American singer Marian Anderson to perform at the Lincoln Memorial in defiance of the Daughters of the American Revolution.
- My mother usually laughed at my father's jokes. Sometimes, she laughed so hard she cried.
- My mother bought me Sara Lee cheesecakes, my favorite, for my childhood birthdays.
- My mother disliked Richard Nixon and defended Alger Hiss and the Rosenbergs.
- My mother, a lifelong Catholic, claimed that Jesus' message in the New Testament was actually pure communism. She said we didn't know whether pure communism would work because it had never been tried.
- My mother owned a collection of classical music on 78s. She told me that when my father proposed to her, she thought he was joking and responded flippantly. Later, she realized he'd been serious. As she worried over how to let him know, she played Mozart's 40th Symphony, her favorite piece, over and over again as loud as she could on her Victrola. My grandmother advised her to call him and apologize for the misunderstanding, which she did. They were married on June 9, 1941.

And finally, this. In a professional portrait of me taken in our home when I was five, I sit on a pink blanket-covered ironing board. I'm wearing a pastel blue rayon dress with a satin belt, white anklets, and black patent leather shoes. My hair is clean and neatly styled. My hands are gently folded on my lap. I'm smiling calmly. Someone had provided the blanket and purchased the dress and shoes. Someone had hired the photographer. These details are captured in the photograph. My mother was responsible for that moment in time.

When she died, I bought a CD of Mozart's 40th Symphony and asked the funeral director to play it during her calling hours. From that music, I infer my mother's inner life, so inaccessible to me. At one time she loved that triumphant, joyful music. I still wish I could have helped her. But I'm learning to express that wish a little differently. I wish, instead, with sadness and love, that my mother could have been happy.

C.S. Lewis to the Rescue

Their prison is only in their own minds, yet they are in that prison.

C.S. Lewis, *The Last Battle*

At the end of C.S. Lewis's *The Last Battle*, the final volume of *The Chronicles of Narnia*, the ultimate battle has been fought and won. Evil has been defeated, and the humans, the dogs, the Giants and all the rest have escaped from the enemy's dark Stable into a new world with a blue sky overhead, fresh air, sweet smells, and blooming flowers. The Dwarfs alone remained trapped in darkness.

The Dwarfs were stuck in the dark hovel, a "pitch-black, poky, smelly little hole of a stable," as one of them grumpily described it. In reality, the Stable had just crumbled to dust around them, and the Dwarfs were huddled together in the midst of the bright sunshine and fresh breeze. They just didn't know it; they believed they were still in darkness. When the God-figure, Aslan, offered them a feast and fine wine, they "thought they were eating and drinking only the sort of things you might find in a Stable," that is, an old turnip and some hay, dirty water, and a bit of cabbage. The desperate Dwarfs fought among themselves over these slim pickings. The efforts of Queen Lucy, Aslan, and the others to show them the light were futile. The Dwarfs remained stubbornly blind.

Like the Dwarfs, I'm attracted to darkness. I like serious movies and books, wince at a contrived happy ending, and indulge in a fair amount of sarcasm and black humor. I worry about what's wrong with the world, enumerate my husband's faults, and obsess over my own failures. I discover uncomfortable connections in Melody Beattie's description of a typical codependent person:

We don't like the way we look. We can't stand our bodies. We think we're stupid, incompetent, untalented, and in many cases unlovable. We think our thoughts are wrong and inappropriate. We think our feelings are wrong and inappropriate. . . We're convinced our needs aren't important.

I see myself in this passage. I have a certain confidence, but low self-esteem is not entirely foreign to me. I'm not sure my mom felt bad about herself, but she certainly felt bad about everything else. She felt alone, unheard, and unloved.

So, at times, have I. I believed that looking at the dark side of things, especially my own dark side, was courageous and realistic. I have let anger at my mom color my relationships with my husband and my children. I've worried that I'm like her. I've blamed myself for neglecting my dying dad and felt ashamed of my childhood, our messy house, and our ill-fated pets. When people have asked me about my family and my mom, I've expressed bitterness. When I hear about a mother who expresses joy at her daughter's wedding or who cries with happiness when her grandchildren are born, I feel resentful. When my kids aren't appreciative, I think to myself, "They don't know how good they have it."

When I have allowed myself to be overwhelmed by these dark thoughts, I haven't done myself any favors. When I have taken up residence in the dark Stable, I've missed out on the happiness around me. I have a husband and children whom I love. We're all healthy. I have a comfortable home and friends and family who care about me.

What's the point of feeling bad so much of the time?

Years ago, I attended an Ash Wednesday service at a local church that combined my parish's congregation with several others. At the entrance to the spacious, modern sanctuary sat a bowl filled with little stones to pick up and hold on to during the service. As it began, we heard the story from John's Gospel concerning the adulterous woman about to be stoned by the law-abiding scribes and Pharisees. They ask Jesus whether they should follow the Law and stone the woman. He says, "If there is one of you who has not sinned, let him be the first to throw a stone at her." The men walk away, one by one, and Jesus tells the woman, "Neither do I condemn you."

In his homily after the reading, the priest described the stones as a metaphor for sin, not the woman's sins, but the executioners'. When we hate someone else and wish to punish them, we're projecting our faults onto them. Instead of throwing their stones at the woman, Jesus advised the men to put down their stones. That is, the men needed to think about themselves rather than about her. They needed to fix themselves.

Near the end of the service, the priest said, we should approach one of the priests scattered around the perimeter of the sanctuary and very briefly confess a fault to him. More precisely, we should describe what we wanted to let go of during the coming Lent. What did we hope to cast away from ourselves? What bad habit, grudge, or shame of our own? As we returned to our seats, we passed by another large earthenware bowl, into which we would drop our stones, symbolically casting off our burden.

You can imagine what my stone represented. I knew immediately when the priest started talking that I was carrying my resentment of my mother in my hand. Yet again, I would try during Lent to forgive her. I would think about her and pray about her. I would contemplate her coolness and rejection and unkindness, her desolate blankness. I would figure her out. If I could understand her, I believed I could forgive her. If I could see her point of view, I'd find her easier to forgive. If I could put her in a sympathetic light, like Mary Doria Russell had done with her fictional torturers, I'd be able to forgive.

At the appropriate time in the service, I approached the priest nearest to me and said I wanted to forgive my mother. He gave me a blessing, and I turned back to my chair, my hand clutching the stone in my pocket. A feeling overcame me as I came near the bowl.

I didn't want to let go of the stone. I didn't want to drop it on the pile. I wanted to keep it. I considered letting it go because that was what we were supposed to do. I imagined I might feel unburdened if I dropped the stone. But, really, I just didn't want to let go of it.

Then I wondered if keeping it in my pocket all during Lent would remind me of my need to forgive. Maybe I should honor my feelings. Maybe what I needed to work on was *why* I wasn't ready to let go. I held onto the stone.

After the service, I walked out of the church with my friend and pastor, Father Dan Begin. He knew nothing of my mother or our history, so I described briefly my quandary and my decision to hang on to the stone. "Here's what I can't let go of," I said. "I keep thinking that I have to see how she was right. But I'm stuck, because I can't see her as right. I think she was wrong."

His response startled me, as his responses so often do. One might expect him to mention shades of gray and point out how rarely one encounters pure right or wrong. But he didn't. Instead, he said at once, "Oh, I'm sure you were right!" I didn't need to change my mind about that, he said, but he implied something else as well, that being right was ultimately irrelevant. Being right or wrong had nothing to do with forgiveness.

I've long since misplaced the stone, but I've contemplated the experience and the words of Father Dan, whose words are always deserving of contemplation. Although I felt my wish to be right was misguided and childish, still, Father Dan's affirmation felt good. At the same time, though, he was calling me to something else that took much longer to comprehend.

It turns out I don't have to understand my mother, exactly, to forgive her. I don't have to keep debating whether I was right or she was right. I have to understand that an illness made her seem cold, invalidating, unkind, desperate and blank. I have to understand that she couldn't help herself.

I had been writing about my mom and Nancy and BPD for months. I began putting pieces together, and they began to take shape, and I began, with fear and trembling, to describe it as a "book." My writing group had read and commented, reacted and helped me. My sisters had read and approved it. I wasn't sure how to tell if it was finished. I wondered how relatives would react. I had written in something of a fury, driven to the computer many days, full of thoughts and insights and memories. I was unsure about the next step, but more at peace about my mom than I'd ever been.

Then I had another dream.

My mom and I were sitting at a table together, not the familiar cluttered kitchen table, but a neat round table. I was showing her a poem I'd written. I don't know what the poem was about, but I was sharing it with her. Something I would never have done in real life.

She was nodding and commenting quietly and listening. She had read the poem, and she liked it. She was making helpful comments. We were sharing this important thing together. This is not something we would ever have done when she was alive. But we were doing it now.

When I awoke and remembered the dream, I felt it strongly. She had read what I had written, and it was okay. My friend Christine insists that my mom, now in some higher place, has worked through her issues and has become who she was always meant to be, and is now able to support and love me. Christine would say my dream was not *about* my mother; it actually *was* my mother.

I don't know. I'm too skeptical and ambivalent to go that far. I'll just say this: after the dream, I felt comforted and reassured. I think, at the least, that my mom would support me if she could.

As Good As It Gets

I divested myself of despair
and fear when I came here.

Now there is no more catching
one's own eye in the mirror,

there are no bad books, no plastic,
no insurance premiums, and of course

no illness. Contrition
does not exist, nor gnashing

of teeth. No one howls as the first
clod of earth hits the casket.

The poor we no longer have with us.
Our calm hearts strike only the hour,

and God, as promised, proves
to be mercy clothed in light.

Jane Kenyon, *Notes from the Other Side*

I go outdoors at midnight to let my dog out. I glance up, where a crescent moon is shining, and the stars are gleaming in a black sky. No clouds—a surprising, blessed occurrence here in Cleveland. I locate the Big Dipper and breathe in the cool night air. Then, I think, how many days have gone by since I've done this? The stars may have been shining every night, but I haven't been noticing.

I dig out an old CD to play. A Beethoven symphony, a Paul Simon collection, or the soundtrack of "West Side Story" or "On the Town." You fill in the blanks with your own favorites. When the music begins, I'm so startled by how good it is, I have to stop what I'm doing and listen, then play it again from the beginning when it's over. How long has it been since I listened to that? How could I have neglected it for so long?

Sometimes I listen, over and over, to Colin Hay's song "Beautiful World," burned on a CD for me by a former student. It has a straightforward melody, beautiful guitar work, and deceptively simple lyrics. "My, my, my, it's a beautiful world," Hay sings, and his verses enumerate all the things he loves. But then, near the end, the words turn dark. "All around is anger, automatic guns, no respect for women or our little ones." These things are real, and "this emptiness persists," he says. There's complexity, shades of experience, not just good emotions and bad emotions, but both at the same time, all mixed together. Perhaps this balance of life's pleasures and life's tragedies, he suggests, is as good as it gets. Here's the ambivalence that my mother seemed unable to comprehend or tolerate.

A favorite song can move you, maybe even change you. Likewise a cherished poem or novel. A photo album shelved for years. A phone conversation with a good friend, or with one's sisters or niece. A great dish, a beloved movie. Flavors and sights and sounds in the world that give you joy. But invariably you forget about them. Then, when you rediscover them, it's a happy experience, if a little bittersweet. Everyone has this experience, don't they?

Maybe not everyone. Early on, when I was just learning about her struggles, Nancy told me something startling. I was, as usual, trying to convince her there was more to life than darkness and pain. "What about joy?" I said. "Joy is just as real as suffering."

"I don't think I've experienced that," she answered matter-of-factly.

At the time, I didn't know how to take this response. I figured she might be exaggerating. Then, not long after, she told me she had never enjoyed a movie or concert all the way through, because at some point she always felt sad or unworthy. At the time, I could hardly take it in, but I have been haunted by this remark ever since.

Nancy's bleakness at first evoked my customary impatience, until I really tried to absorb it, to believe what she was saying. Never to enjoy a movie fully. Never to lose oneself at a concert. Never to feel joy. In Roger Lewin's *Fusing and Losing*, he quotes another therapist as saying, "Why don't they enjoy the things about life that I enjoy? I can't understand it. It's like not liking chocolate. But they don't."

New life springs up around the huddled Dwarfs, and a delicious feast is set before them. They not only can't *enjoy* the experience, they can't even *have* the experience.

Nancy is her own unique self, but she also serves as a medium for my mother. She's a skilled translator—more self-aware, expressive, introspective, analytical, and higher functioning than my mother, although she'd reject all these adjectives. I try to grasp that my mother may never have felt joy. Or, at least, never after my father's illness. I wasn't with her all the time, but my mother's old records remained dusty and untouched in their cabinet. As far as I know, she never once listened to Mozart's 40th Symphony in the last forty years of her life.

"No one involved with a borderline," writes Janice M. Cauwels, "is alone in feeling bewildered, anguished, furious, and helpless." Yes, exactly. Bewildered. Anguished. Furious. Helpless.

In a roundabout way, though, my mother has made me a happier person. It may seem contradictory, since I have complained here for many pages. My particular Christian faith tells me that it's not so strange, though, to find a deeper happiness grow out of bewilderment, anguish, fury, and helplessness. This is what Mary Oliver calls a gift in a boxful of darkness.

Recognizing how much my mother's unhappiness pained me

and my sisters teaches me how my own unhappiness might affect others. Maybe, forgiving her and becoming happier myself help not only me, but everyone around me as well. In *Eat, Pray, Love*, Elizabeth Gilbert claims, "All the sorrow and trouble of this world is caused by unhappy people." She perceives that in her own life, her unhappiness has at times distressed those around her. She says,

> *The search for contentment is, therefore, not merely a self-pre-serving and self-benefiting act, but also a generous gift to the world. Clearing out all your misery gets you out of the way. You cease being an obstacle, not only to yourself but to anyone else. Only then are you free to serve and enjoy other people.*

When you're looking at somebody else's dark Stable, it's much easier to cherish your own light, the occasional sweet-smelling violet, and cool breeze. My mother has, ironically, helped me dispel some of my darkness. Her misery has wiped off what Melody Beattie calls the "dirty, brownish-gray film" on my glasses and made them a little rosier.

It's all about perspective, and mine is changing all the time, even as I write. My blog friend Michael, for example, has offered me a new take on my own book's title. He reminds me about *ha-martia*, the Greek term for an archer's missing the target, which has also been used as a definition of *sin*. He suggests that's what I mean by *missing*. He says, "It wasn't directly your mother's fault she failed you," because her illness made her unable to hit the mark. I tell him I never thought of *missing* in that sense, because it never seemed to me she was even aiming, but now I realize maybe she was. Maybe she loved us just like we love our kids, like Betsey and Marge loved Karen and Chad, like Ceres loved Proserpina. All the sadder then, that her love got all twisted up inside of her and couldn't be expressed. "It's only when you get to the depth of your mother's problem," Michael responds, "that you realize love isn't anything like what we imagine."

As a result, it hasn't been so hard, recently, to feel that I'm forgiving my mother. She was so sad. How futile to hold a grudge against someone so sad. I still want her to be happy, but there's nothing I can do about it now. If there's an afterlife, I hope she's happy there. She suffered enough. I hope that, right now in eternity, she could be narrating Jane Kenyon's elegant "Notes from the Other Side." I hope she has no illness. I hope she has divested herself of despair.

I hope she has met God and is basking in "mercy clothed in light." I hope her heart, at last, is calm.

Acknowledgments

Deepest thanks to my writing group, which started up, miraculously, just as I was beginning to write the disjointed fragments that eventually became this book. Roberta Jupin and Christine Lang, AKA "The Midwives," provided wisdom, cogent criticism, and awesome patience. Thanks to Conchy Fajardo-Hopkins for her early reading and helpful reactions. When Oprah calls, you all will be the first to hear.

Father Dan Begin's enthusiastic reading and intuitive understanding of my purpose were a precious gift. Thanks to friends Leanne Lombardo, Jan Thrope, Jean Andolsen, Mary Powell, Barbara Bolek, Kathie Ellis, Robin Koslen, Joanne Westin, Laura Tayyara, and Tricia Dykers Koenig for early reading and encouragement. Marianne Sachs shared her kind heart, sensitive intelligence, and empathetic spirit with me. Thanks to Chris Wellman for her exquisite rendition of an Avon fan rocker. Heartfelt appreciation goes to my blog readers and Internet friends Mary Smith, who put me in touch with the very helpful Dr. David M. Allen; and Michael Whitely, whose insights I've shamelessly cribbed.

Thanks to Doreen Kelleher for unceasing moral support and for sharing her lovely book group with me.

Peter Collopy and Zelda MacGregor were skilled advisors on matters technical.

My sisters Betsey Jarc and Marge Baker and my nieces Stephanie Baker and Brigitte Belmonte-Jarc made invaluable contributions. Their fact-checking and corroborative memories helped so much, as did their loving support and sense of humor.

For publishing advice, thanks to Fred Collopy and Franklin Hickman. Rita Grabowski at Cleveland State University's Poetry Center was especially generous with her time and attention. Cristina Bryan at Barclay Bryan Publishers lent me unexpected and much-appreciated encouragement.

Marian Sandmaier gave generously of her time in reading and responding to my manuscript, as did Gerald Sindell. Dr. Barbara Finn lent her expertise, reading closely and commenting astutely—all this for a stranger with no psychological training.

Heather Summerhayes Cariou, author of *Sixtyfive Roses: A Sister's Memoir*, provided both encouragement and bracing criticism. Perry Hoffman of the National Education Alliance for Borderline Personality Disorder and Clea Simon, who wrote *Mad House: Growing Up in the Shadow of Mentally Ill Siblings*, also offered welcome guidance.

Jewel Moulthrop deserves her own appreciative paragraph, both for her meticulous editing and generous heart.

I'm indebted to Dave Megenhardt and Red Giant Books for turning this into a real book.

I treasure the Michael Schwartz Library at Cleveland State University and its connection to Ohio Link.

My husband John Ewing, editor extraordinaire, provided careful readings as well as moral support. He has borne my long ruminations on borderline personality disorder with forbearance and compassion. Despite that chapter about him, he is most emphatically not a jerk. Thanks also to Doug and Margaret for their patient listening and compassionate reading.

I can never thank my friend "Nancy" enough. Her resilience and honesty inspire me every day.

References

Melody Beattie. *Codependent No More: How to Stop Controlling Others and Start Caring for Yourself.* New York: Harper & Row, New York, 1987.

Beck, Aaron T., and Arthur Freeman. *Cognitive Therapy of Personality Disorders.* New York: The Guilford Press, 1990.

Berry, Wendell. "To My Mother." *The Selected Poems of Wendell Berry.* Berkeley: Counterpoint Press, 1998.

Bloomgarden, Andrea. "Dialectical Behavior Therapy," *Comparative Treatments for Borderline Personality Disorder.* Springer Publishing, 2004.

BPD Sanctuary. < http://www.mhsanctuary.com/borderline/ BPDtherapist/63.HTM>.

Burroughs, Augusten. *The Wolf at the Table: A Memoir of My Father.* New York: St. Martin's   Press, 2008.

Cauwels, Janice. M. *Imbroglio: Rising to the Challenges of Borderline Personality Disorder.*   New York: W.W. Norton & Co., 1992.

Chapman, Alexander L., and Kim L. Gratz. *The Borderline Personality Disorder Survival Guide: Everything You Need to Know About Living with BPD.* Oakland: New Harbinger Publications, 2007.

Clarkin, John F., Frank E. Yeomans, and Otto F. Kernberg. *Psychotherapy for Borderline Personality.* New York: John Wiley & Sons, Inc., 1999.

Cloud, John. "The Mystery of Borderline Personality Disor der." *Time,* 8 January 2009.

Drabble, Margaret. *The Radiant Way.* New York: Alfred A. Knopf, 1987.

Finn, Barbara. "Affectional Need in Pyschotherapists as a Countertransference Issue: Borderline Patients," Ph.D. dissertation, 1985.

Freeman, Arthur, ed. *Comparative Treatments for Borderline Personality Disorder.* New York: Springer Publishing Company, 2005.

Friedel, Robert O. *Borderline Personality Disorder Demystified: An Essential Guide for Understanding and Living with BPD.* Marlowe & Company, 2004.

geordieger. "borderline, or extreme (Borderline Personality Disorder)." http://www.dooyoo.co.uk/archive-lifestyle/ borderline-personality-disorder/287510/

Gilbert, Elizabeth. *Eat, Pray, Love: One Woman's Search for Everything across Italy, India, and Indonesia.* New York: Viking, 2006.

Gunderson, John P. *Borderline Personality Disorder: A Clinical Guide.* Washington: American Psychiatric Publishing, Inc., 2008.

Harper, Robert G. *Personality-Guided Therapy in Behavioral Medicine.* Washington: American Psychological Association, 2004.

Heller, Sharon. *The Vital Touch: How Intimate Contact with Your Baby Leads to Happier, Healthier Development.* New York: Henry Holt and Company, 1997.

Kathy Ewing was born and raised in Northeast Ohio. She has written on topics including education, books, women's issues, and dogs, for such publications as Belt, The Bark, The Book Group Book, The Plain Dealer, Great Lakes Review, and Growing without Schooling. She has taught at all levels, from nursery school to college, and currently teaches Latin at Cleveland State University and writing at Case Western Reserve University. She has two grown children and lives in Cleveland Heights with her husband John Ewing. She blogs at www.kathyewing.com.

CPSIA information can be obtained
at www.ICGtesting.com
Printed in the USA
LVHW031503041221
705284LV00006B/399